FROM
COVER
TO
COVER

FROM COVER TO COVER

Evaluating and Reviewing Children's Books

KATHLEEN T. HORNING

HARPERCOLLINSPUBLISHERS

For Jay and Marie,
who read to me

From Cover to Cover

Evaluating and Reviewing Children's Books

Copyright © 1997 by Kathleen T. Horning

HarperCollins Children's Books, a division of HarperCollins Publishers,
10 East 53rd Street, New York, NY 10022.

Library of Congress Cataloging-in-Publication Data

Horning, Kathleen T.

   From cover to cover : evaluating and reviewing children's books / Kathleen T. Horning.

      p.   cm.

   Includes bibliographical references.

   ISBN 0-06-024519-0. — ISBN 0-06-446167-X (pbk.)

   1. Book reviewing.   2. Children's literature—History and criticism.   I. Title.

PN98.B7H67   1997   96-27281

028.1'62—dc20   CIP

Typography by Gail M. Hess

1   2   3   4   5   6   7   8   9   10   ❖   First Edition

Acknowledgments

The idea for this book was first suggested to me by my friend Ruth Gordon, librarian, writer, anthologist, and an extraordinary critic in her own right. I would like to thank her for suggesting it and for trusting me to do it.

The work could not have been completed without the fine children's literature collections at the Cooperative Children's Book Center, a library of the School of Education, University of Wisconsin—Madison, and at Madison Public Library.

My colleagues at the Cooperative Children's Book Center have enthusiastically offered their support and encouragement. I am indebted to Director Ginny Moore Kruse, my friend and mentor, who has guided my professional growth from the first day I entered the CCBC; and to Megan Schliesman, who has greatly enriched the workplace with her intellect, insight, and good humor. Regular participants in the CCBC's monthly book discussions have generously shared their time and their opinions about new children's books. I would especially like to acknowledge Anne Altshuler, Elizabeth Askey, Philip Heckman, Eve Robillard, and Joan Thron, who, month after month, continue to add their distinctive voices to our discussion.

My colleagues at Madison Public Library help me

keep my feet on the ground at all times with their astute professional observations about books and children. It is my privilege and pleasure to work with Director Barbara Dimick and with children's librarians Geri Cupery, Katherine Odahowski, Linda Olson, and Pam Wittig. Also, I would like to thank the children themselves, who have, knowingly or unknowingly, helped me to see books through their eyes. I have been especially enlightened over the years by: Alyce, Anna, Arvina, Erin, Khalidwe, Oliver, Lina, Dameeka, Georgina, Javier, Kent, Melissa, Li Li, Andreas, Lydia, Finn, Nora, Claire, Hannah, Anders, Danny, Neara, Toby, Shayle, Stuart, Sophie, Reggie, Malcolm, and Gianna, and their respective parents.

My friends and colleagues in other fields who generously share their perspectives and wisdom continually broaden my understanding of children's books. I would especially like to acknowledge and thank my good friend Margaret Jensen, a brilliant teacher who brings trade books into her classroom and proves, year after year, that there is a great reader inside every child.

CONTENTS

INTRODUCTION

With 5,000 new books for children being published every year, it may seem an overwhelming task to wade through them. But with this embarrassment of riches, it is important for adults who work with children and books to sharpen their critical skills so they can select the best books available. But how do we determine which books are the best ones? What makes a good children's book? Are there simple standards we can apply across the board? Or are there different sets of standards for different types of books? Or for different needs or audiences? This book is meant to serve as a beginning place for those who want to evaluate or review books published specifically for children. It will provide concrete examples of aspects to consider when looking at children's books with a critical eye.

DISTINCTIONS BETWEEN EVALUATION AND REVIEW

For our purposes, we will use the term **evaluation** to refer to a critical assessment of a book—in other words, the thought process one goes through in order to formulate an opinion of the book. Sometimes book evaluation can be done very quickly, drawing on a wealth of professional or personal experience; other times it requires a great deal of deliberation, careful thinking, perhaps even consultation with outside sources of information. This book will offer guidelines for evaluating the various genres of children's books: nonfiction, folklore, poetry, picture books, beginning readers and easy chapter books, and fiction. It will also offer advice on how to write a review.

Review refers to a formal written expression of the critical assessment, generally printed soon after the book under consideration has been published. Good reviews help readers create a mental picture of the book by briefly describing it and presenting an assessment of its quality.

WHAT MAKES A GOOD CHILDREN'S BOOK?

There are no quick, easy answers to this question, because there are so many different kinds of children's books that can be outstanding for different reasons. Furthermore, as times change and our perception of children evolves, so too do our standards for excellence in children's books. Each chapter in this book will open with a brief history that will help to provide a context for the type of book under discussion, followed by evaluative criteria, using examples from outstanding books. Newcomers to the field may wish to seek out these exemplary books to expand their general knowledge of children's literature by reading some of the best books we offer children.

CHAPTER 1

A Critical Approach to Children's Books

Reading a book for the purposes of evaluation and review requires more attention to detail than reading a book for personal pleasure or for information. When you read to evaluate, your assessment of the book will ultimately affect other potential readers. It may make a difference as to whether or not a book is purchased for a library or school or as a birthday gift for a child you'll never meet. In fact, it may make a difference as to whether or not the book is read by a child at all. It is your professional responsibility to try to take your evaluation beyond a personal response.

This is not to say that your personal response doesn't matter. It would be impossible, of course, for you to put it completely aside—you are a reviewer, after all, not a robot! What the responsible reviewer strives for is an informed and reasoned opinion, clearly articulated so that others can learn about books they haven't seen.

In essence, a children's book reviewer reads and writes with two audiences in mind: (1) adults who read reviews to help them select books for children and (2) the children themselves. It may also be read by the author and publisher of the book in question; however, neither is the intended audience for your review. In other words, it is not your goal to write a review to stroke an author's ego or to pick a bone with a publisher.

Still, it is important to remember that most books for children are created with the best intentions in mind. No one sets out to produce a crummy book that kids will hate. If this is your initial assessment of a book you're reviewing, it would be unfair and unwise to let it stand as your final one without a great deal of further consideration. You'll need to take a closer look at the book. What was the author's intent in writing the book? What qualities did the editor see that led her to believe that the book merited publication? Why did the illustrator choose this particular style? The answers to all these questions have their origins in the history of the book's creation. While it isn't necessary for you know the details of a book's publishing history in order to review it, an understanding of the general context in which children's books are created will help you read more critically.

HOW CHILDREN'S BOOKS ARE PUBLISHED

Many publishing houses have divisions or departments that are especially devoted to publishing books for young people. These were, for the most part, established in the 1920s and developed through the pioneering efforts of women such as Louise Seaman Bechtel, May Massee, Helen Dean Fish, Marian Fiery, and Virginia Kirkus, who were the first children's book editors. Unlike adult book divisions, which are driven by the consumer market (bookstore sales), children's book divisions developed largely in response to an institutional market. Sales to libraries and schools accounted for a high percentage of the total number of children's books sold. As library budgets began to shrink in the 1970s and 1980s, children's book publishers began to turn their marketing toward consumer sales as well, although the institutional market continues to be an important influence in the children's book industry.

There are books that are created specifically for one market or the other. Those that are produced for the institutional school market alone are called *textbooks*. They are generally sold to entire school districts rather than to individuals. They are also created in a separate division of the publishing industry that specializes in producing books to fit the exact needs of teachers working with specific school curricula and guidelines at various grade levels. Books that are produced with only the consumer market in mind are called *mass-market books*. These are generally produced as paperbacks or as picture books with inexpensive cardboard covers (such as Little Golden Books), and they may be sold in supermarkets, airports, dime stores, and convenience stores as well as bookstores. While there are publishers that specialize in producing mass-market books, most children's book departments produce mass-market books to some degree.

Books created for both the consumer market and the institutional market are called *trade books.* These are sold to schools and libraries. They are also sold directly to consumers through bookstores. Both quality and child appeal are taken into account when weighing the sales potential. From the publisher's point of view, the best kind of children's trade book is one that will succeed in both the consumer and the institutional markets and will continue to sell well for decades. This is the type of success guaranteed to a book that wins the Newbery or Caldecott Medal.

Most children's books start out as an idea in the mind of an author. That may seem obvious to you, but I mention it here because many people seem to have the notion that ideas start with publishers, who then assign them to authors. I often hear people ask children's editors: "Why don't you publish more books about X?" in a tone that suggests they hold editors personally responsible for the lack of X books. But editors don't tell authors what to write. They must wait for X to develop in the mind of the author, and then they have to determine if it's good enough to publish. The editors' role is to find and nurture the talents of authors and artists who will create good children's books. If they cast their nets wide enough, their catch may include an author who will come up with the idea of writing about X on her own.

Once a manuscript is accepted for publication, the editor works with the author to help shape the book into its final form. An editor may make suggestions about chapters that need to be rewritten, characters that need to be developed, or ideas that need to be clarified. The ultimate responsibility for the writing, however, rests with the author. If the author has submitted the text for a picture book and she is not an illustrator herself, the editor will choose an artist to illustrate it. While the author may see preliminary sketches of the illustrations along the way, chances are that the author and illustrator will never meet while the book is in production. Generally the author has very little say about the illustrations other than factual content.

When the final version of the manuscript is completed, the editor—in conjunction with the design and marketing departments—will estimate the number of pages there will be in the printed book, specify the *trim* (size of page), and decide the type of binding and the number of copies to be printed for the initial print run (the quantity expected to sell within a set period of time). She will also discuss jacket art with the art director, who will in turn assign the work to an artist if it is not an illustrated book; most picture-book jackets are illustrated by the artist doing the interior art. Again, the author generally has little or no say in such matters. The manuscript is turned over to a *copy editor*, who will read it to correct spelling, grammar, and inconsistencies in style and internal plot. A copy editor may question noticeable errors in fact but will not retrace every step of an author's background research. In most cases the author has final say about the copy editor's changes.

Next, the manuscript is turned over to a *designer*, who

will choose an appropriate *typeface*. Based on the number of *characters* (letters, numbers, spaces, and punctuation marks) in the final manuscript, the designer will choose a typeface that will fill the number of pages the editor estimated earlier. He may have some sample pages printed out at this point so that the editor can look at the *page layout* (what the printed page in the book will look like) and decide if the type and page design are appropriate for the look of the book. The size of type in a children's book is especially important, as it often dictates the age level of the book's audience. Children are surprisingly sensitive to typeface. If they decide it's too small, they're likely to reject a book as "too hard," no matter the content. If they decide it's too large, they may scoff at a book as "babyish."

When the editor and designer have made the final decisions about typeface, number of lines per page, margins, and other design elements, the manuscript is turned over to the production department for the final stages of the process. The production department will arrange to have paper, chosen for its color, weight, and cost, and material for the binding, often chosen to coordinate with the jacket, sent to the printer. A compositor will set the type and initially prints the book in *galley proofs*. An author rarely makes any substantive changes in the text at this point, although the author, editor, and a proofreader will look at the proofs carefully in case there are any printer's errors or any blatant mistakes that were somehow missed earlier.

Because of the visual nature of picture books, they undergo a different production process. After an artist has been commissioned to illustrate a picture book, he discusses layout and design with the editor and art director, and makes preliminary decisions about how each page will look. Next he prepares and submits *roughs*, detailed pencil sketches for each page spread. Once the roughs are approved, the artist completes and delivers the finished artwork for the book. The designer prepares a camera-ready *mechanical* that shows the position of text and illustrations and includes instructions for the printer. The first set of color proofs come back from the printer, and they are carefully checked against the originals by the artist, art director, and editor, so that any problems with color, size, and position of the illustrations can be corrected. When these final decisions and adjustments are made, and after a few more proof stages for final checking, the book goes off to be printed and bound.

In the meantime, the editor has enthusiastically described the book to the company's in-house sales representatives at the seasonal sales conference. They will in turn try to get the book into bookstores across the country. The publisher's marketing and promotion department have been working on behalf of the book as well. Above all, they want to get the word out to the world at large that the book exists. They will write a glowing description of the book to put into their seasonal catalogue. They will include the title in announcement ads of the season's forthcoming books that appear in trade journals such as *Publishers Weekly* and *School Library Journal.* They may choose to buy advertising space in a children's literature review journal to specifically highlight the book. Or they may create posters, bookmarks, flyers, or buttons advertising the book to give away to librarians and teachers at professional conferences.

They will also send out advance *review copies* of the book (often specially printed from uncorrected first galley proofs, so reviewers can evaluate the book early) to professional journals and to some general publications. In addition, review copies are sent to large library systems and departments of education for their own internal review. Favorable reviews and recommendations for purchase by these large systems can be important to the success of any given children's book, since institutional sales still account for a significant part of the children's tradebook market. In fact, throughout most of the twentieth century children's librarians have set the critical standards for children's trade books. The ultimate prizes for children's authors and illustrators are, of course, the Newbery and Caldecott Medals respectively. These are the only book awards that have a nationwide impact on sales, and they are given annually by children's librarians under the auspices of the American Library Association.

THE PARTS OF A BOOK

Just as a bit of background about the publishing industry can help to inform your reading, so too can an understanding of the book itself as an object. Although books may vary widely from one another, there are several constants in the way they are designed that should be familiar to you. It's useful to know the special vocabulary of the book—to know what endpapers are, for example, or what is meant when someone refers to flap copy. As a critical reader, you should be aware of all the parts of a book that contribute to the whole. You may even find a piece of information in the author's acknowledgments or on the copyright page that will help you with an assessment of the book.

Beyond the body of the book proper, created by the author and/or illustrator, we can look at three additional parts: *binding*, *front matter*, and *back matter*.

BINDING

The cover: Children are notorious for judging books by their covers, and that, of course, is the opposite of what the critic strives for. Most hardcover children's trade books come with a paper *dust jacket* that includes color artwork designed to entice potential readers. The part of the jacket that folds around the inside of the cover is called a *flap*, and it contains printed information, known as *flap copy*. The front flap generally gives a brief summary of the book and typically concludes with a lot of superlatives about how great the book is, while the back flap often includes biographical information *(bio)* about the book's creator(s).

Professional reviewers don't always see the dust jacket, as they often see books before they are published, in a form known as *bound galleys* or *prepublication copies*. Whether you see the jacket or not when you are evaluating a book, it is important to keep in mind that jackets function more as part of a book's marketing and promotion than as an integral part of its art.

Most children's trade books make their first appearance as *hardcover* or *clothbound* books. (These two terms mean the same thing and are used interchangeably.) The hard covers themselves are composed of heavy cardboard stock covered with cloth or paper, or a combination of the two. *Library bindings* on hardcover books are reinforced to stand up to multiple circulations, whereas *trade bindings* are on books produced primarily for bookstore sales. If a hardcover book sells reasonably well, the publisher may choose to issue a *paperback* edition or may sell the paperback rights to another publisher. In some cases a publisher opts for *simultaneous publication* and issues a hardcover and paperback at the same time. Other times, a hardcover edition will be skipped altogether and the book will be issued as a *paperback original*. Because they generally fall into the category of mass-market books, many paperback originals are not taken seriously by reviewers and are only briefly noted or even completely overlooked, though they are regularly purchased by libraries. Most popular series books, such as "Choose Your Own Adventure," "Baby-Sitters Club," and "Goosebumps," are issued as paperback originals and thus have rarely withstood the scrutiny of professional evaluation and review.

Endpapers: Every hardcover book has sheets of paper, generally of heavier stock, pasted flat against the insides of the front and back covers and along the *gutters* (the page edges at the inside margins) of the first and last

pages of the book. Sometimes endpapers include supplementary information, such as maps, and sometimes—particularly with picture books—they are illustrated or the
story actually begins and ends on the endpapers. More
often than not, however, endpapers are left blank,
although they may be of a color contrasting with or complementary to the cover or jacket, to add to the overall
aesthetic of the book.

FRONT MATTER

Half title: The first page of a book, bearing only the
book's title, with no author or publisher listed. Half-title
pages are carryovers from the past, when books were sold
without bindings and half titles served to both identify
and protect the pages stacked in bookshops.

The back, or *verso*, of the half-title page sometimes lists
an author's previous books. This is called an **ad card**.
Illustrated books sometimes use the verso of the half-title
page for an illustration known as a *frontispiece*. Sometimes
books are designed so that this page forms a double-page
spread with the **title page**.

Every book has a title page, and it contains some of
the most important information about the book. Both
sides of the leaf are considered to be part of the title page.
The front, or *recto*, includes the full official title of the
book, including a subtitle (if there is one); names of
people associated with the creation of the book, such as
the author, illustrator, adaptor, or translator; an editorial
imprint; and the name of the company that published the

book. The title page recto sometimes includes, in addition, the year of publication and information about the edition.

The other side of the title page, or the **title page verso**, is often chock-full of small print that reveals a great deal about the production of the book. Because of all the information related to the book's *copyright* on the title page verso, this page is even more often referred to as the **copyright page**. The year of original publication is shown in the copyright date, which follows the symbol ©. Referring to the copyright statement should be part of every critic's routine, because it helps to establish a context for the book you are about to evaluate. Was the book originally published in another country or in an earlier edition? If so, the copyright statement will tell you. When more than one date is listed after a copyright, the one that corresponds to the book you are holding in your hand is always the most recent year, since editions are necessarily published in chronological order. This is the date you will cite in the bibliographic information accompanying your review.

Publishers generally include information related to a book's printing history on the copyright page as well. People sometimes use the terms *printing* and *edition* interchangeably; however, they are not technically the same thing. *Edition* refers to all the copies of a book printed from the same sets of plates. There may be several *printings* of a single edition, but except for occasional minor changes such as the correction of a misspelling, there are not significant textual differences between printings. You may see a notation on the copyright page such as *First Edition,* which generally means the book you are holding is the first printing of the first edition, in other words the first appearance of this particular text. The notation *First American Edition* is often a sign that the book was first published in another country. When that is the case, you may see a statement such as "First published in . . ." which will tell you the country of origin, the date of first publication, and the original publisher of the book. If parts of the book were published elsewhere previously (such as in a magazine), as is often the case with collections of poetry and short stories, this should be indicated on the copyright page as well, or on a continuation of that page.

Many publishers also include a printing code here, showing the number of printings a particular edition of a book has been through. In printing codes, the numerals 1–10 may run backward or forward or may show the even numbers running forward, followed by the odd numbers running backward. Whichever way the numbers appear, the lowest one that appears in the code tells you the number of the printing of the book you are holding.

For example, 2 4 6 8 10 9 7 5 3 1 is a standard code for a first printing. Note that the lowest number in this string is 1 —that's how we can tell the book is a first printing. Using the same style of code, a fourth printing would be 4 6 8 10 9 7 5. The numerals 1, 2, and 3 have been dropped from this string. Another publisher might designate a first printing with 10 9 8 7 6 5 4 3 2 1 and a fourth printing as 10 9 8 7 6 5 4.

Today most books published in the United States also

include *Library of Congress Cataloging-in-Publication data* (CIP) on the title page verso. The CIP resembles a tiny library catalogue card and includes the book's author, illustrator, title, series title, ISBNs, subject headings, Dewey classification, year of publication, and for children's fiction books a one- or two-line summary of the book. Like the dust jacket, however, the CIP should never be taken as an integral part of the book. The book creators themselves have no control over this information; therefore, books should never be criticized for misinformation in the CIP. The *International Standard Book Number* (ISBN) is an important piece of information that appears here (and usually with the bar code on the back of the book); each binding of each title has a unique ISBN, to be used in placing purchase orders. Trade bindings, library bindings, and paperback editions of the same books all have separate ISBNs, which should be indicated in every review's bibliographic citation.

Other valuable details related to a book's production are sometimes found on the title page verso. You may find, for example, an author's source note for a folktale. If photographs have been used to illustrate the book, photo credits often appear here. In picture books some publishers now indicate the illustration media on the title page verso, and in books of all kinds, names and sizes of type styles used are sometimes cited, in addition to the name of the book designer.

The following page often consists of the author's and artist's **dedications** of the work to one or more individuals. Like jacket art, flap copy, and CIP summaries, dedications are generally irrelevant to the assessment of the book as a whole. Sometimes an author thanks someone who has been helpful in the book's creation, and this sort of information should be included on the **acknowledgments page**, which sometimes follows the dedication page or sometimes appears at the end of the book. Unlike dedications, acknowledgments can be significant to the critic: It is quite common for writers to seek out the expert opinions of content specialists, who read over the final manuscript of a book prior to publication and point out any inaccuracies or implausiblities they notice. This sort of acknowledgment by the author usually indicates the content specialist's professional affiliation. Helen Roney Sattler's book *Hominids: A Look Back at Our Ancestors* (Lothrop, 1988) includes the acknowledgment "I am especially grateful to Dr. James McKenna, chairman, department of anthropology, Pomona College, for reading the completed manuscript and for offering valuable suggestions and information along the way, as well as for checking the drawings for accuracy." This tells us that although the author is not herself an anthropologist, a specialist in the field had a hand in the book's creation, and it may be of help in assessing accuracy.

Preface: A short note, written by the author, includes details about the creation of the book that are not an essential part of the book's content. Sometimes called simply an *author's note*, it may give readers a brief description of what inspired the author to write the book, or it may tell us why the author believes the subject of the book is important. In children's books we sometimes see a variant of this called "A Note to Parents." This typically includes information about the levels of understanding children are likely to possess at different ages. For example, Joanna Cole's book about human reproduction, *How You Were Born* (Morrow, 1993), includes a note for parents that outlines the types of questions young children have about the subject and suggests how parents can best answer them.

Foreword: Like the preface, a foreword is also a short note about the book's creation and the need for information on the topic; however, a foreword is written by someone other than the author, often an expert on the book's subject.

Table of contents: Books with chapter headings include a table of contents that lists the chapter headings in order and indicates the page number for the beginning of each chapter. The table of contents can be especially helpful in a nonfiction book, because it often reveals the organization (or lack thereof) of the material in the book. In novels chapter titles listed in the table of contents may provide a quick summary of the action, which can help you remember plot details after you have read the book.

Between the table of contents and the body of the book, the publisher may insert another **half-title page**. If the book is divided into two or more named parts, there will be a **part-title page** here, right before the beginning of the body of the book. This may simply say "Part One" or "Book One," or it might give a specific title to the section, such as "The Escape."

BACK MATTER

Additional information often appears at the end of the book, as well, particularly in works of nonfiction. Back matter can be an essential part of the book, and it should be evaluated and reviewed as carefully as the body of the book itself.

Epilogue: A brief concluding statement that stands apart from the text as a whole. There is often a sense that the author has made a sudden jump ahead in time from the body of the book. Judith St. George's biography *Crazy Horse* (Putnam, 1994) ends with the subject's death in 1877. The short epilogue that follows tells the reader that there is no record of where Crazy Horse was buried and that much about his life has remained a mystery.

Afterword: A short and usually subjective passage in which the author shares his or her own personal responses related to the subject of the book.

Appendix: Supplementary or summarizing material on a particular aspect of a nonfiction topic is sometimes included in an organized section at the back of the book. A book on the history of major-league baseball, for example, might include an appendix providing a chronological listing of World Series winners. Appendices are typically labeled by letters—A, B, C, and so on—followed by a descriptive title:

> Appendix A: World Series Winners
>
> Appendix B: All-Time Record Holders

Glossary: An alphabetical list of words and expressions, used in the body of the book, that may be unfamiliar to readers. Each entry in a glossary is defined, and sometimes a pronunciation is included as well. Glossaries are usually confined to the special vocabulary related to the subject of the book. A glossary in a book on a ballet company, for instance, might include words such as "arabesque," "barre," and "pointe."

Source notes: In nonfiction, source notes or *references* provide readers with a record of the original sources the author consulted while researching the topic. Source notes may be listed chapter by chapter, in the order in which the information is cited in the text. Authors sometimes include a sentence or two to give readers insight into the research process used and how decisions were made when sources conflicted with each other.

Bibliography: The original sources consulted by the author are also generally listed alphabetically by the author in a bibliography. In books for the young, authors sometimes provide, in addition, a bibliography of *books for further reading* that lists books on the subject that are written at roughly the same age level as the book in hand.

Index: An alphabetical list of topics and/or names that appear in the body of the book, accompanied by the page number(s) on which the item can be found.

Bio: Biographical information about the author sometimes appears on the very last printed page of the book. This may be a restatement of the back-flap bio, or it may be an expanded version.

CATEGORIES OF
CHILDREN'S BOOKS

We typically categorize children's books in two ways: by *age level* and by *genre* or type. Juvenile trade publishing produces books for all ages of children from babies up through the teen years. The age level of the intended audience generally dictates both form and content.

Nonfiction, or books of information, as they are often called, is published for all ages. But two books on the same topic, even written by the same author, will be very different from each other if one is aimed at three-year-olds and the other is written for children ages eight to ten. It stands to reason that a book on human reproduction published for preschoolers will differ greatly from a book on the same subject published for adolescents. The age level of the intended audience may also dictate subject matter. A book on going to day care would obviously be for preschoolers, a book on the history of the Negro Leagues of baseball for older readers.

Folklore and **poetry** are also published for all ages of children. As in nonfiction, both style and content will differ according to the age level of the intended audience. Many picture-book editions of single folktales are published every year, some for children as young as two or three and some for children as old as eight or nine. Collections of folktales and other kinds of traditional literature, such as mythology, tall tales, and epic literature, are generally aimed at school-age children. Young children, who respond naturally to rhythm and rhyme, are a receptive audience for nursery rhymes and humorous verse, the early roots of poetry. Older children enjoy humorous verse as well, in addition to more sophisticated forms of true poetry, some of which is especially written for children and some selected from poetry written for adults.

In the area of **fiction**, specific forms have been created to meet the unique needs and interests of children at various ages. **Picture books** have been especially developed as an art form with young children in mind. These thirty-two-page creations ingeniously combine words and pictures to tell stories preschoolers want to hear again and again. **Easy readers** are the next step up from picture books. They are consciously created to help build the skills of children who are just learning to read. **Transitional books** move up one step more to serve as a bridge between easy readers and children's novels, often called **chapter books**. At all levels children's fiction covers a range of subjects, themes, and styles and represents some of the best writing we find in the world of literature today.

In the upcoming chapters we will take a closer look at all these categories. Each one merits special consideration and requires a slightly different approach. Since this book is especially intended for people who are new to the field of children's books, I will provide a brief history of the different types of children's books as they have developed in U.S. trade publishing, so that you can get a sense of how these books came to be. In discussing critical standards, I will use examples from well-known and easily available books, which also represent some of the best books of their types. You may choose to seek out some of these books so that you can read them to build your familiarity with the literature.

Throughout the book I will suggest questions you can ask yourself as you go on to evaluate books on your own. These questions are intended not as a test, but to help you begin to make concrete critical judgments about what you are reading. Some of the questions may already seem obvious to you. If so, that's good! You are well on your way to being a critical reader and a responsible reviewer. As you gain experience with book evaluation, these sorts of questions will become second nature to you.

Finally, there is no substitute for reading widely yourself. The more experience you have as a reader of children's books, the easier it will be for you to think about the one you have just read. One of the most important skills you can acquire is the ability to place a book in an appropriate context. How does it measure up against others of its type? *Are* there, in fact, others of its type? Or is this something fresh and new? One of the greatest thrills for a children's book reviewer is to find the book that is truly innovative and groundbreaking, or completely satisfying and close to perfect. That's what keeps us all reading.

Books of Information

Nonfiction is an essential part of every child's library, whether the child reads it for specific information, recreation, or both. Many children prefer to read nonfiction exclusively, and they may voraciously read through every children's book a library owns on the subject of horses or ancient Egypt or basketball. Young readers sometimes go through phases where they will read only biographies, for example, or books about dinosaurs. Some children like to browse through highly visual books of information, pausing to read captions and perhaps a bit of corresponding text when a certain picture grabs their attention. Others trek to the library looking for books on a particular topic they have been assigned to report on at school. Whatever their motivation for reading nonfiction, children deserve to have books of information that are accurate, engaging, and well written.

The past several years have seen great changes in

children's nonfiction, many of which may be traced to the mid-1980s. After languishing throughout the 1970s due to cuts in federal funding, which previously had supported school library purchases of nonfiction (science in particular), nonfiction made a comeback after several titles were cited as Newbery Honor Books. The impact of the Newbery Medal cannot be underestimated in twentieth-century children's literature published in the United States. Because it is the only literary award that actually has an impact on sales nationwide, the Newbery Medal strives to set the standard for excellence in children's books. It also seems to have an impact on what sorts of books get published; unfortunately, it rarely honors nonfiction, a fact that was brought to the public's attention in 1976 by Milton Meltzer's widely read *Horn Book* essay "Where Do All the Prizes Go?: The Case for Nonfiction."

Although the Newbery Committee had recognized nonfiction prior to this time, it was not until the mid-1980s that the honors came more frequently. The 1983 book *Sugaring Time* (Macmillan), a photoessay by Kathryn Lasky and Christopher Knight, won a Newbery Honor. Two years later the Newbery Committee named Rhoda Blumberg's *Commodore Perry in the Land of the Shogun* (Lothrop, 1985) as an Honor Book, and the following year the 1986 science book *Volcano: The Eruption and Healing of Mount St. Helens* (Bradbury), by Patricia Lauber, was cited. Finally, in 1988, the Newbery Medal was awarded to a nonfiction book for the first time in over thirty years—to Russell Freedman's *Lincoln: A Photobiography* (Clarion).

While there has always been excellent nonfiction published

for children, these four books stood out not only for their distinguished writing but for their eye-catching presentations. *Volcano*, for example, was one of the first photo-essays to use color photographs. Today it would be hard to find a children's photoessay that didn't! *Lincoln* was generously illustrated—so much so that the word "photobiography" was invented for the subtitle, to call attention to this fact in the book's subtitle, lest potential readers dismiss the book as just another dull, thick black-and-white biography. All these books stand out as examples representing two forces at work: The American population, including both children and adults, was being seen as more "visually oriented," that is to say, more responsive to pictures than printed words, and changes in technology allowed publishers to indulge this belief. Almost overnight we began to see newspapers and magazines decrease the number of printed words they were using and increase the numbers of illustrations. In publications for children this trend had the biggest impact on nonfiction. We began to see books of information relying more on illustration, with many book creators successfully using unconventional approaches. The books in Joanna Cole and Bruce Degen's innovative "Magic School Bus" series are a good example.

Another change recently introduced is that nonfiction is being aimed at younger and younger children. Books of information are now being published for preschoolers, some for children as young as two years old. This suggests a conscious move away from the idea that nonfiction books are mostly "homework" books. Interestingly, some small children, like their older peers, show a definite preference for books of information, or "books with real stuff," as they call them. Others just as happily accept a mixture of fact and fiction, if their adults are openminded enough to offer them nonfiction as well as storybooks. And a lot of books of information for preschoolers serve a dual purpose and function as a bridge between adult and child, informing two generations simultaneously. The books in Fred Rogers' popular "First Experiences" series are clearly aimed at two-year-olds, and yet they also acquaint parents with what a toddler is likely to need to know about starting day care or making friends or going to the doctor.

With all the variety in approach and content found in these books of information, not to mention the needs, abilities, and interests of the young readers themselves, there are still critical standards that can be applied across the board in the evaluation of children's nonfiction. You need not be a subject specialist yourself to evaluate them, but you do need to be a careful and critical reader. Approach the book with a questioning mind as you think about its accuracy, organization, illustrations, design, prose, and documentation.

AUTHORITY
AND RESPONSIBILITY
OF THE AUTHOR

The first question to ask yourself as you approach a book of information is: Who is the author? It may be a name you know and recognize as a reputable writer of information books for children, or it may be a name you have never seen before. Check for an author bio at the back of the book or on the back flap to try to determine what sort of authority the author has. Biographical information often reveals that an author has an educational background related to the subject about which he or she is writing. This is not to say that an author *must* have a formal education in a particular field in order to write about it; it is merely the first step the responsible critic takes in a systematic evaluation of a book's accuracy. By the same token, you must not assume that an author's subject expertise guarantees success in writing for children, even if he has written outstanding children's nonfiction in the past. Again, an assessment of the author's authority is just one piece of critical information you may use in building your evaluation of a book.

Check the acknowledgments next to see if the author has cited the name of a content specialist who read the manuscript for accuracy. This is an especially important step for writers who do not have a background in the subject about which they are writing; and even those who do often wisely seek the informed opinion of another expert. The children's nonfiction writer often walks a fine line between making a subject comprehensible to children and simplifying to the point of inaccuracy. A content specialist can call an author's attention to areas in which he is in danger of having crossed over into the realm of inaccuracy. Beyond assuring accuracy, the acknowledgment of expert advice shows that the author respects young readers and believes that it is important that they have access to accurate information.

Another indication that the nonfiction writer respects the needs of young readers is the use of inclusive language and illustrations. By this we mean that boys *and* girls of all racial backgrounds should feel included, rather than excluded, from the social life of the book. Both text and illustrations should show a realistic diversity of different types of people. An excellent example of how an author or illustrator's responsible choices in this area enhance the material is *Hominids: A Look Back at Our Ancestors* (Lothrop, 1988), written by Helen Roney Sattler and illustrated by Christopher Santoro. Both the author and illustrator have avoided the white-male bias that has been prevalent in studies of human evolution for decades simply by taking a broader—and more realistic—view of the human family. Beginning with the use of the anthropologically accurate term "hominid" instead of the popular term "early man," Sattler is careful to use language that specifies gender only when gender is significant in her discussion (the height of a female *Australopithecus afarensis* vs. that of her male counterpart). Similarly, Santoro's black-and-white line drawings show males and females in equal number, and when drawing comparisons between ancient hominids and contemporary humans, people of all races are shown as the norm.

Of course there will be instances in nonfiction when the subject matter dictates that only one race or gender be represented. One would not expect to see women gratuitously included, for example, among the signers of the U.S. Declaration of Independence, nor would one expect to see Norwegians present during the construction of the Great Wall of China. But the vast majority of topics covered in the field of children's nonfiction can be approached with a wide vision. There is no excuse in this day and age for a children's book of science experiments, for example, to show only white boys with test tubes.

ORGANIZATION

The way in which information is organized in books for young readers is of utmost importance. A good nonfiction book arranges material in a logical sequence. The two most common organizational patterns in books of information for children are *enumeration and chronological order.* In enumeration the author describes the relevant parts of a subject in some sort of orderly fashion. Schoolchildren themselves learn to enumerate when they are taught to organize information for reports by first making a topical outline. Chronological order is the obvious pattern for history or biography, but it can be used to illuminate other subjects as well. By choosing a chronological arrangement for *The Hungry Woman: Myths and Legends of the Aztecs* (Morrow, 1984), compiler John Bierhorst brilliantly demonstrates the relationship between myth, legend, and history in addition to providing a distinctively Aztec perspective on the arrival of the Europeans into their world.

Before you begin to read any nonfiction book, you should look at it critically to see how it is organized. In longer books of nonfiction, a table of contents often provides a clear picture of a book's organization. Take, for example, the table of contents in James Cross Giblin's *From Hand to Mouth: Or, How We Invented Knives, Forks, Spoons, and Chopsticks & the Table Manners To Go With Them* (Crowell, 1987):

1- Flint Knives and Fingers
2- Ancient Spoons and Knives
3- Don't Put Your Whole Hand in the Pot!
4- The Quick Little Fellows
5- The Fork Comes to the Table
6- The Rise and Fall of Table Manners
7- Forks in Tokyo, Chopsticks in Chicago

Even with Giblin's playful chapter headings and without dates cited, we can ascertain that his book is arranged chronologically.

Now let's take the table of contents for Milton Meltzer's *Poverty in America* (Morrow, 1986):

1- Money Makes a Difference
2- Taking the Measure
3- Breadlines and Soup Kitchens
4- Living in the Streets
5- It's Not Only Me
6- Growing Up Poor
7- Women in the Job Ghetto
8- How the Elderly Live
9- When a Farm Dies

Just by looking at the chapter titles in this table of contents, you can see a logical order in Meltzer's arrangement of his subject matter: Chapters 1 and 2 provide a general introduction to the subject; chapters 3 and 4 discuss the effects of poverty; chapters 5 through 10 describe categories of Americans most affected by poverty; and chapters 11 through 13 put the problem into a historical context by discussing responses in the past, present, and future.

Many shorter books for young children have a straight narrative that is not broken up into chapters. That doesn't necessarily mean that the books lack logical organization. A common pattern in books of information for young children is to begin with the familiar and move to the unfamiliar. A book for young children on the subject of tigers, for example, might start out with house cats, a common animal familiar to most children, and then move by extension to the less familiar animal, tigers. This technique takes into account what children are likely to know at a particular age and uses their common knowledge as a foundation, moving from familiar to unfamiliar, from known to unknown.

Atsushi Komori's outstanding science book *Animal Mothers* (Philomel, 1979) is exemplary for its organization of simple information aimed at two- and three-year-olds.

Each double-page spread in this book shows a different animal mother and how she moves her babies from one place to another. This information could have been arranged willy-nilly in the book and, with its stunning realistic illustrations by Masayuki Yabuuchi, it would have been just as appealing to toddlers, and yet Komori's excellent organization of the material makes this a true science book. As simple as the book is, with just one short sentence per page, you can still outline the information as it appears in the book to reveal a logical arrangement by which each page builds on the one that appeared before it:

    I. Mother carries baby
        A. in mouth
           1. cat
           2. lion
        B. on body
           1. baboon (baby clings to mother's stomach)
           2. chimpanzee (mother carries baby in arms)
           3. koala (baby rides on mother's back)
           4. sloth (baby rides on mother's stomach)
           5. kangaroo (baby rides in pouch)
    II. Baby walks independently
        A. elephant (mother pushes baby with trunk)
        B. zebra (baby follows behind mother)
        C. wild boars (babies follow mother in a bunch)
        D. hedgehogs (babies follow mother in straight line)

Whenever you set out to evaluate a book of information, you should always try to get a sense of the book's distinct parts and how they are related to each other—in other words, how the information is organized. Shorter works that are not divided into chapters might at least have internal headings that will set off the various parts of the text. The distinct parts should, at the very least, be clear to you as you are reading the book, and if they're not, this is likely an indication that the author has not succeeded in clearly organizing the material for a young audience.

One final type of organization of the book's material is with an alphabetical index that appears at the end of the book. Good indices give readers access to specific pieces of information within the body of the text. Indices are usually prepared by professional indexers, not the author of the book, although the author has the chance to approve an index.

ILLUSTRATIONS

As children's nonfiction has become more and more visual over the past decade, illustrations have become a more essential part of the overall structure. Many of the finest recent books of information engage young readers by asking them to look for some specific thing in an accompanying illustration. In Patricia Lauber's lavishly illustrated *The News About Dinosaurs* (Bradbury, 1989), for example, the author calls the reader's attention to a realistic color illustration of a fossil showing small sauropod footprints surrounded by large ones. She goes on to tell us that this evidence suggests that, unlike reptiles today, dinosaurs may have cared for their young, as the fossil record shows us that young sauropods were kept at the center of a group when a herd moved from one place to another. In this case the illustration is being used not only to illustrate the author's point, but to draw children into the scientific process by showing how scientists draw theories from observations.

Color photographs are being used today in a great number of science books to convey information that would be otherwise inaccessible. Seymour Simon has used the extraordinary photographs made available by NASA expeditions over the past decade in his recent books about astronomy. In *Our Solar System* (Morrow, 1992), for example, the photographs themselves enter into the scientific investigation of the planets, as Simon discusses the conditions under which they were taken and what scientists have learned as a result. Bianca Lavies uses the technique of microphotography to give children a closeup view of small worlds in books such as *Compost Critters* (Dutton, 1993).

Recent advances in photo reproduction have opened the door to a popular subgenre of children's nonfiction: the photoessay. These books combine text and photographs to give readers a "you are there" sense and cover a wide range of subjects, from a typical day in the life of the raptor rescue center in St. Paul, Minnesota, to the contrasting lives of a Palestinian boy and a Jewish boy living in Jerusalem. Author-photographer Susan Kuklin has set the standard for excellence in this genre. Since 1984 she has produced photoessays on a wide variety of topics for children from preschool through the teen years; all are based on primary research through interviews and observation, documented by her photographs. In *Kodomo: Children of Japan* (Putnam, 1995), for example, she describes typical days in the lives of seven school-age children living in Hiroshima and Kyoto. Kuklin chooses her subjects carefully so that they represent her topic, and yet she always allows for enough diversity, so a single person does not carry the responsibility for representing everyone.

Color reproduction in books has become so sophisticated lately that it is quite easy to be bowled over by a book's dazzling illustrations. It is important, however, not to lose sight of the main purpose of illustrations in a book of information: to provide information by complementing, supporting, or extending the text. Look closely at a book's illustrations to determine what exactly they add to the work. How do they relate to the text? Are they merely decorative, or do they actually enhance the text in some way? Do they make the subject matter more appealing? Are they up to date? Are captions clear and accurate? Do the captions add supplementary information or repeat what's in the text?

DESIGN

We often speak of book design in terms of overall aesthetic appeal, but when it comes to nonfiction, design becomes an important aspect of getting information across to readers. In addition to making the subject seem more inviting, the design of a nonfiction book can be used to clarify the sequence of ideas and to show how the parts are related. Headings and subheadings can be set off in different type sizes and styles to illuminate the organization of ideas.

The artist-naturalist Jim Arnosky uses design to his advantage in his many "how-to" drawing books. Take a look at *Drawing Life in Motion* (Lothrop, 1984), for example, to see how he consistently uses two different typography styles throughout to provide different levels of information. As a result, he successfully integrates two simultaneous narratives: his role as observer and his role as artist. Thanks to design, his points of reference are always clear to young readers.

Design is a big factor in the success of the "Magic School Bus" series by Joanna Cole and Bruce Degen. Open to any page in a book from this series and note the various strands of information operating simultaneously through text, dialogue, and student reports. In *The Magic School Bus Lost in the Solar System* (Scholastic, 1990), for example, a fourth strand is introduced with the teacher, Ms. Frizzle, occasionally reading from her lesson plans, and this is clearly marked off from other dialogue simply through the use of pink lined paper as the background of her dialogue bubbles. There is a lot going on on every page of the books in this series, and an innovative design not only allows this to make perfect sense, but also permits story to function as science and fantasy at the same time.

A fully integrated, successful design does not call attention to itself, so the critical reader must look closely at all the elements of book design to see how it works.

Look first at the typography. Is the type size appropriate for the intended audience? Children are very sensitive to the size of a book's type. Large type and shorter line length make text more readable for children in third and fourth grade, but by the time a child is in fifth grade, large type signals that the book is for "babies," and no self-respecting fifth grader would be caught dead with it. These same children are put off, however, by a sea of type: a medium-sized typeface with lots of white space on each page suits them best.

In addition to type size, look at style. Are different styles or sizes used consistently to get across different kinds of information? If headings and subheadings are used, do they appear in different type sizes, or are subheadings bulleted or indented to set them off from headings?

Look at the placement of illustrations. Do they generally appear next to the part of the text that discusses what they picture, or do readers have to do a lot of flipping back and forth to match text with pictures? Do they frequently break up the flow of the text, or do they enhance it?

WRITING STYLE

While background research, organization and structure, design, and illustrations are all used to present information to children, writing style ultimately brings the subject to life. Clear prose that engages the reader, stirs the imagination, and awakens the mind is every bit as important in works of nonfiction as it is in fiction. When the author has a certain passion for the subject matter, that enthusiasm is transferred to the reader through writing style.

Laurence Pringle is a master at writing dynamic prose in his science books for children. In doing so, he makes his subject matter more interesting by demonstrating the nature of scientific inquiry, or what many writers refer to as the "scientific attitude." In his introduction to botany, *Being a Plant* (Crowell, 1983), Pringle gives basic information on his topic; he also acts as an intermediary between popular beliefs and the theories of modern science, and presents scenarios in which scientists come into conflict with each other. Yet his prose is always clear and concise. Consider, for example, the way in which Pringle lays the groundwork for introducing the concept of geotropism in *Being a Plant*:

> *Plant stems grow up and roots grow down. But how does a plant tell up from down? And then, what causes it to grow in the right direction? Botanists have long wondered about these questions.*

He begins with a simple declarative sentence that even a three-year-old would understand. Then he plants two questions in the minds of readers that arouse curiosity and provide a structure for their intellectual approach to information in subsequent paragraphs. Finally, he suggests that this information is the result of an on-going scientific inquiry. In spite of the simplicity of the language Pringle uses, he does not talk down to his young readers. His tone shows that he has respect for their intelligence.

In the above-quoted passage from *Being a Plant*, Pringle enlivens his prose by using a conversational tone made up of everyday language, includes questions, and occasionally addresses the reader directly by using second person. The author's mood toward both subject and audience is expressed through tone. In nonfiction we see a range of tones used successfully. A humorous tone is the hallmark of Joanna Cole's "Magic School Bus" books and is employed, as well, in David Macaulay's book *The Way Things Work: From Levers to Lasers, Cars to Computers— A Visual Guide to the World of Machines* (Houghton, 1988) without diminishing the book's informational value. Here is how Macaulay describes the mechanics of a typewriter:

> *Like the piano, the typewriter also contains a system of levers that converts the small movement of a fingertip on a key into a long movement—in this case the movement of the raised type on the end of the type bar. As the typewriter is always played* fortissimo, *a simple system of levers suffices to connect the keys to the type.*

Unfortunately, in lesser hands attempts at a humorous tone in informational books for children fall flat and the books end up sounding condescending or just plain silly. But when authors know their subjects well and have respect for the intelligence of their audience, a humorous tone can add a great deal of appeal to a book of information.

Helen Roney Sattler's book *Hominids* uses a neutral tone by presenting its information matter-of-factly, as can be seen in the following example:

> *Since these hominids apparently did not make stone tools, there is not much evidence to suggest the way they lived. They may have hunted small game—lizards, eggs and such. But like* A. africanus, *they were obviously the hunted more often than the hunters. More than half of those that have been found died before they reached adulthood. Their average age was eighteen. All of their bones and most of the animal bones found with them had been gnawed by large predators such as saber-toothed cats, hyenas, or leopards.*

Note the precision and clarity of Sattler's language as she presents and interprets evidence from the fossil record. Her use of words such as *apparently, may,* and *suggest* provides a constant reminder of the theoretical nature of science. It also signals a distinction between fact and informed opinion, and demonstrates the nature of true scholarship.

An author who cares deeply about his subject matter

may take a partisan tone in nonfiction. In his powerful social histories for young readers, Milton Meltzer is known and respected for the strong partisan tone he takes. Writing about his book *Never to Forget: The Jews of the Holocaust* (Harper, 1976), he comments: "Terrible and complex as the events were, they can be brought within the range of understanding if the reader is helped to see them from the inside. If a reader can be made to feel, to care, he or she will be much more ready to see them from the inside."

Walter Dean Myers skillfully uses matter-of-fact descriptions of historical events to support and explain his partisan tone in *Now Is Your Time!: The African-American Struggle for Freedom* (Harper, 1991).

> *What was it like to be called a slave? What was it like to be "owned" by someone? There is no single answer to this question. There is the common experience of being considered inferior, of being bought and sold as if one were a horse or household furniture. Many people who sold Africans would often add a few household items to the sale so that they did not appear to be "slave dealers." Most plantation owners did not seem to realize that the Africans hated the very idea of not being free. (George Washington, in*

*August of 1761, complained that his
Africans ran away without cause.)
But the best way to find out what it
was like to spend a lifetime in bon-
dage is to read the documents from
those days.*

Myers then goes on to present primary evidence from
first-hand accounts written in the nineteenth century in
reports, letters, reminiscences, and business statements,
allowing readers to, in Milton Meltzer's terms, see "from
the inside."

To evaluate the writing style in nonfiction, it may be
helpful to ask yourself the following questions: Is the
prose clear and dynamic? What kinds of words and sentences are used to get the ideas across to young readers?
Does the author use a creative or original approach to the
subject matter? Does the text present principles and concepts, building on a logical development of ideas, rather
than merely reciting facts and figures? What sort of tone
does the author use, and is it appropriate for the subject
matter? Is this a book one would want to read aloud to a
child or group of children?

DOCUMENTATION OF SOURCES

By documentation we generally mean a bibliography of
sources that were consulted by the writer doing background research. Documentation can also refer to the use

of footnotes or endnotes that cite sources for direct quotes and specific pieces of information.

Most bibliographies of sources that were consulted as background research appear at the back of the book. Source material can be divided into two categories: primary and secondary. The use of primary sources indicates that the author has done original research, which is uncommon but not unheard of in children's nonfiction. Glennette Tilley Turner combined primary and secondary research in her extraordinary biography *Lewis Howard Latimer* (Silver Burdett, 1991). Because so little had been written about this African-American inventor, Turner turned to primary sources, such as unpublished papers in the Schomburg Center for Research in Black Culture at the New York Public Library. She also conducted over twenty personal interviews with content specialists and members of Latimer's family. In her bibliography Turner divides the sources into categories: Books; Newspapers and Journals; Unpublished Materials; and Interviews.

Photoessays that use the photodocumentary technique are, by definition, based on primary research. The photographs themselves, in addition to personal interviews woven into the text, provide the author's documentation. One would not expect to find a bibliography of sources in this sort of photoessay unless the author has brought in additional information from secondary sources.

Most writers of children's nonfiction rely on secondary sources, such as books and articles that have been written by others on the topic. Take a look at the sources listed. Are they up-to-date? Do cited articles appear in popular magazines such as *Newsweek*, or do they come from scholarly sources? One of these is not necessarily superior to another, but a critical look at sources may give you a picture of the depth of the writer's expertise in the subject.

Another type of bibliography that frequently appears at the back of children's nonfiction is a list of suggested or further reading. These titles are generally aimed at young readers, and it is sometimes unclear whether they were sources actually used by the author in his or her own research. Some bibliographies integrate adult and children's material, and when they do, they often indicate which titles would be appropriate for young readers — in plain listings of titles, a symbol such as an asterisk may be used; in annotated bibliographies, the descriptions of the books include such information.

Many authors also include endnotes that document sources of direct quotations used in the body of the book. The practice of using footnotes, or citations that appear at the bottom of the page on which the quote appears, is rare in children's books, most likely because it is considered to be more of an academic convention than part of the art of nonfiction writing.

Notes from the author at the back of the book sometimes truly seem to be a type of documentation that is aimed at child readers as well as adults. The highly regarded biographer Jean Fritz often uses endnotes to provide supplementary information on a particular topic or to point out to readers accounts that disagree. For example, in her biography of Elizabeth Cady Stanton, *You Want Women to Vote, Lizzie Stanton?* (Putnam,

1995), Fritz explains in a note why Lucretia Mott's husband, James, chaired the Women's Rights Convention in 1848 and that sources disagree as to whether he served as chair during both days of the convention or just on the second day. She could have included this information in the body of the text but chose not to break up the flow of the text with a digression.

Many critics of children's nonfiction feel quite strongly about the documentation of sources, and yet there doesn't seem to be any clear consensus as to what level and type of documentation should be used. There is more agreement among adults about *why* information should be documented than *how* authors should do it, and the most common reason given is: for the benefit of child readers. If that is the case, then perhaps Sue Macy sets the best example for creating child-friendly documentation in her excellent history of the women's professional baseball league, *A Whole New Ball Game: The Story of the All-American Girls Professional Baseball League* (Henry Holt, 1993). Macy's source notes are written as a brief essay in which she describes the steps she took in doing her research, discusses the sources she used, and tells us which ones were most helpful. Next she includes a description of nonprint sources of information for children who are interested in the history of the league, including motion pictures, museums, and sources for collecting All-American Girls Baseball League baseball cards. Finally, she provides an annotated bibliography of books for further reading, categorized by subject.

While the documentation of sources is clearly an

important factor in evaluating nonfiction, the success of a book should not rise or fall based solely on its citations or lack thereof. Of all the factors I have described that make up a nonfiction book, documentation is clearly the easiest to assess: Either it's there or it isn't. For this reason, I suspect that some critics who are willing to write off a book due only to a lack of documentation are opting for the easy way out. They are disregarding some of the more challenging questions: What is the author's authority? How is the material organized? Does the design clarify the sequence of ideas? Do the illustrations extend the text? What sort of writing style does the author use? The answers to all these questions, and more, ultimately add up to the success or failure of a book of information. We at least owe it to our audience of readers to consider them all as we evaluate nonfiction.

CHAPTER 3

Traditional Literature

Traditional literature is a general term that applies to myths, epics, legends, tall tales, fables, and folktales that originated in oral storytelling and have been passed down from one generation to the next. The original authors of these tales are unknown, although today the stories themselves have sometimes come to be associated with the name of the person who first collected the oral version and wrote it down. Thus, much of the folk literature of Europe, for example, is attributed to the Brothers Grimm, who were among the first scholars to record the tales as ordinary people told them in the early nineteenth century.

The act of collecting oral stories for the purposes of recording them is an academic pursuit; for the past century and a half it has been a particular preoccupation of anthropologists who wish to preserve the stories for scholarly cultural studies. Most of the traditional literature from non-European sources was initially collected for these purposes, not as a potential source of entertainment for American children.

How is it, then, that contemporary American children's literature abounds with traditional literature? There seem to be several factors at work. First, there is a long tradition of myth, legends, and folktales being served up as children's literature. With the European fairy tales, for example, while children were undoubtedly part of the audience for the oral tales in their original context, they were not the sole, or even primary, audience. But once the tales were written down, they gradually came to be seen as the province of children, due to many of the common characteristics they share that make them very appealing and accessible to children: concentrated action, stock characters, patterned language, elements of fantasy, and simple themes, such as good vs. evil and the weak overcoming the strong and powerful.

A second factor that has encouraged the link between traditional literature and children's books is the emphasis on oral storytelling as a part of library programming for children. Librarians trained as storytellers quite naturally seek out stories from traditional oral sources as likely candidates for their own retellings. This creates a demand for publishing in this area, which in turn makes critics from the children's library field fairly welcoming and receptive to a wide range of traditional material being published as children's books.

Third, with the increasing demand for multicultural literature, there has been a tremendous increase in the amount of traditional literature from non-European sources over the past ten years or so. Lyn Miller-Lachmann attributes this to the fact that folktales offer advantages to those who wish to expand multicultural literature: ready-made characters and plots that can be extracted from sources in the public domain that require no royalty payments. But children's book editor Phoebe Yeh cautions that retelling and illustrating folktales from other cultures raises complex issues of authenticity. She points out that it is naive to assume this is the "safest" way to increase the number of multicultural books.

A final factor that contributes to the abundance of traditional literature in contemporary U.S. publishing for children has to do with the power of the stories themselves. Many of them are exceptionally good stories, plain and simple! Who cannot identify with the growing vexation of the Baby Bear upon finding his porridge eaten, his chair broken, and an intruder in his bed? Who cannot be moved by John Henry's valiant but unsuccessful attempt to race a steam drill? Ultimately, the tales have survived for their sheer power as stories dealing with universal human truths.

CLASSIFICATION OF TRADITIONAL LITERATURE

Scholars agree on several different categories of traditional literature, and these definitions can be useful to anyone evaluating traditional literature for children. The first step to take as you evaluate a traditional story is to determine the category into which the tale falls. This will not only help in your overall approach to the book as you read and critique it; it will also allow you to use more precise language when you express your opinions of the book.

Here are the most common categories of traditional literature:

MYTHOLOGY

These stories explain the existence and nature of the world, and generally feature gods and goddesses as their primary characters, although mortals occasionally put in an appearance. Myths are often considered to be sacred stories in their culture of origin.

EPICS

Long, episodic stories of adventure, grounded in mythology but featuring a mortal hero. The best-known epics in the Western tradition are *The Iliad* and *The Odyssey*.

LEGENDS

Stories based on supposedly real people and their heroic deeds and adventures. Part of the intrigue of legends is that their characters, such as King Arthur and Johnny Appleseed, are said to have a historical basis, and yet their stories are a mix of fantasy and reality.

TALL TALES

A type of legend in which the hero's exploits are highly exaggerated and retold in a hyperbolic style, generally to the point of being hilariously funny.

URBAN LEGENDS

A recently identified type of contemporary oral tale that recounts bizarre or supernatural occurrences, sworn to be true as the teller generally claims the event happened to a friend of a friend. In spite of their name, they can be set in any real place, urban or rural. These tales are popular with older children, as well as teenagers and adults, and are beginning to make their way into published literature for children.

FABLES

Very short stories that teach a moral or a lesson about conduct. Fables rarely feature more than two characters, and the characters are often animals.

FOLKTALES

Fanciful short stories with either human or animal characters. Most folktales have fast-moving plots in which good is eventually rewarded and evil is punished. Folktales themselves have been divided into several categories:

Cumulative: Stories such as "The House That Jack

Built," which are structured with the repetition of an ever-increasing accumulation of details.

Pourquoi: Stories that explain the origins of natural traits, such as "Why Mosquitoes Buzz in People's Ears."

Beast tales: Stories in which animals talk and behave as people.

Fairy tales: Also called "magic tales" or "wonder tales," stories with elements of magic and enchantment. They may include supernatural characters such as witches, wizards, elves, dragons, and even, occasionally, fairies.

Realistic: The rarest type of folktale, these are stories with human characters and no magic elements.

As you evaluate any book based on traditional literature, one of the first things you should do is to determine the *tale type*. Is the story a retelling of a myth? Is it a legend? Or pourquoi tale? Sometimes this information will be given to you in the book's subtitle or in an author's note, but most often you will have to make this judgment yourself by applying what you know about the categories of traditional literature. Among children's literature professionals the above-named categories are widely known and understood, so your use of these descriptive terms in published reviews will be especially helpful.

Traditional stories from all these categories are published in the United States for children each year, although the vast majority of these are folktales. Many are published individually, a single story presented in one thirty-two-page picture book; others are published as collections of tales in one volume. Whatever the mode of presentation, there are critical standards that can be applied to all traditional literature when it is being retold for a child audience. These standards relate to the context in which the literature is created: first, as an oral literature that undoubtedly changed as it was passed from storyteller to storyteller; next, as it was consciously collected and recorded for posterity; and finally, as it was taken from one written source, reshaped, retold, and recreated into another as a book for children.

ORIGINAL SOURCES

The evaluation of traditional literature begins with a healthy dose of curiosity about the original source of the material. Ask yourself: Where did this story originate? Because very few writers of children's books have primary contact with the actual source of an oral story, they must generally rely on a printed version that was collected for another purpose by another person.

In recent years there has been a growing demand that authors who retell traditional literature for children cite the printed sources from which they derived the story. In her excellent article "Cite the Source: Reducing Cultural Chaos in Picture Books," the critic and folklore scholar Betsy Hearne has evaluated the methods authors currently use for citing sources in picture-book folktales and has found that they fall into five different categories:

1) Model source notes cite specific source(s) and provide a description of the cultural context in which the story was told, as well as a description of any changes the author made in his or her retelling;

2) **Well-made source notes** cite the specific source(s) in a highly visible presentation at the beginning or end of the book, and may also include cultural details related to the story;

3) **Fine-print source notes** cite specific source(s) in a less visible manner, generally in small print on the book's title page verso;

4) **Background-as-source notes** give general information about the culture from which the tale comes and sometimes information about the story itself, without citing a specific printed source;

5) **Nonexistent source notes** provide no information on sources at all beyond, perhaps, a subtitle such as "An Old Tale" or "A Navajo Legend."

Dr. Hearne goes on to argue convincingly that as critics we should consider types 4 and 5 completely unacceptable. She writes: "[I]t's time to declare that part of a great picture-book folktale *is* the source note, that context is important to text."

Source notes are invaluable to the critic. Beyond assessing the level and quality of the note itself, you may choose to seek out the original source to compare it to the book you are evaluating. This is an especially important step to take when the tale is previously unknown to you or when it comes from an unfamiliar culture or tradition. By comparing the adaptation to the original, you can determine the quality of the author's retelling. What details have changed? Is there a logical reason for any

changes, omissions, or additions? Has the author successfully re-created the original tone of the story? What elements reflect the author's own style?

Kevin Crossley-Holland's model source notes for the
retellings in his book *British Folk Tales: New Versions*
(Orchard, 1987) offer capsule histories of the tales themselves, so that even tales that are familiar to readers can
be read with new eyes. Look, for example, at his source
note on the well-loved story "Goldilocks and the Three
Bears":

The Doctor by Robert Southey (1837)

*The earliest known version of this
nursery tale was written down by
Eleanor Mure in 1831, but I have
chosen to follow the clean lines and
formulaic repetitions of Southey's version. Southey, however, described his
visitor to the three bears as a "little old
Woman" with an "ugly, dirty, head";
I have bowed to more recent taste . . .
in changing her into Goldilocks—a
form she first took in 1904* (Old
Nursery Stories and Rhymes, *illustrated by Joan Hassall) after passing
several incarnations, including Silver-
Hair (1849), Silver-Locks (1858) and
Golden Hair (1868). I have also
dropped most of Southey's moral
asides. . . .*

Crossley-Holland's version of "The Three Bears" includes several details not commonly found in other retellings: The bears are all male and are described as "the great, huge bear," "the middle bear," and "the little, small, wee bear" rather than the more familiar Papa Bear, Mama Bear, and Baby Bear. Goldilocks expresses her frustration with the words "Bother and bother!" and "Dash and dash!" When the bears return home, they find evidence of an intruder through clues Goldilocks has left behind: spoons left in porridge bowls; chair cushions left flattened and out of place; pillows and blankets rumpled on the bears' beds. These details have generally been omitted from other retellings, in which the three bears seem to know instinctively that someone's been eating their porridge, sitting in their chairs, and sleeping in their beds. Lastly the Crossley-Holland version ends with one further formulaic repetition: As the bears examine their beds, each of their voices enters into Goldilocks' dreams. The great, huge bear's voice is like thunder rumbling; the middle bear's voice is like ". . . somebody speaking in a dream"; and finally the shrill, high-pitched voice of the little, small, wee bear wakes her up.

A quick consultation with Southey's version, which can be found in Iona and Peter Opie's *The Classic Fairy Tales* (Oxford, 1974), reveals that most of these details came directly from the original source. Goldilocks' interjections were Crossley-Holland's invention, but the description of the bears, the trail of evidence, and the effect of the voices on a sleeping Goldilocks were all part of the 1837 version. By comparing his version to the original, we can see that Crossley-Holland's skill comes through in his deliberate decisions based on thorough research and in his lucid retelling, which restores the story's original charm.

Other retellers have strayed a bit farther from the source in their retellings of "Goldilocks and the Three Bears" but have come up with equally enchanting versions. Byron Barton's version, *The Three Bears* (Harper, 1991), take a minimalist approach by scaling the text down to the least number of words that can be used to tell the story. His concise text is well matched with boldly colored, uncluttered illustrations, making the edition perfect for very young children who are hearing the story for the very first time. James Marshall's text in *Goldilocks and the Three Bears* (Dial, 1988) adds many humorous asides; on noticing a lot of coarse brown fur around the bears' house, for example, Goldilocks surmises, "They must have kitties." The author, too, adds occasional comments himself, in the spirit of Dr. Southey's moral asides. Marshall's tone, combined with his wry illustrations, makes it clear that he is inviting children to laugh at Goldilocks' bad manners and errors in judgment, mistakes they themselves would *never* make. His edition is ideal for children who are already familiar with the story and who are thus likely to enjoy Marshall's unique additions.

NARRATIVE STYLE

The most successful retellings of traditional stories for children maintain something of the flavor of their oral origins.

As Betsy Hearne has pointed out, these stories should come alive when they're read out loud: repetition, rhythm, and robust sound are often important features in oral stories.

Julius Lester is especially gifted as a teller of tales from African-American traditions and is perhaps one of the best writers when it comes to capturing the sound of oral storytelling in written form for children. Lester achieves this by using short sentences, natural dialogue, humorous exaggeration, and surprising metaphors, and by occasionally addressing his audience directly.

> *The next day John Henry went to town. He met up with the meanest man in the state, Ferret-Faced Freddy, sitting on his big white horse. You know what he was doing? He was thinking of mean things to do. Ferret-Faced Freddy was so mean, he cried if he had a nice thought.*
>
> *John Henry said, "Freddy, I'll make you a bet. Let's have a race. You on your horse. Me on my legs. If you and your horse win, you can work me as hard as you want for a whole year. If I win, you have to be nice for a year."*
>
> *Ferret-Faced Freddy laughed an evil laugh. "It's a deal, John Henry." His voice sounded like bat wings on tombstones.*

Julius Lester's narrative is not only easy to read aloud; it is also easy for listeners to understand and follow, due to his faithfulness to oral traditions.

In his Iktomi stories, Paul Goble uses three different typography styles in an attempt to re-create a traditional Lakota storytelling style. In a preliminary note to the reader in *Iktomi and the Boulder* (Orchard, 1988), for example, Goble states:

> *Iktomi's thoughts, printed in small type, need not be read aloud but can perhaps be read when looking at the pictures with children. Readers may even have their own ideas to add about what Iktomi is thinking.*
>
> *Where the text changes to italic, readers may want to let their listeners make remarks about what Iktomi is doing. This is quite in keeping with traditional Iktomi story-telling; listeners are expected to make their own comments and rude remarks about Iktomi.*

Many storytellers choose to take on a more formal tone in their retellings to reflect the serious nature of the tale they are telling. But even with stories of this kind, the original oral style is generally direct and to the point. Note, for example, the style of the following Lenape tale from John Bierhorst's collection *The White Deer, and Other Stories*

Told by the Lenape (Morrow, 1995), recorded directly from an oral source, Lenape elder Nora Thompson Dean:

> *Well, this is a story about a squirrel. At one time he was a very huge creature, and he went about the lands on the prairies—and the woods. He killed everything he saw, and he would eat these different animals—the lynx, and the weasels, and wolves, everything he'd catch— he would eat these creatures.*

Compare that authentic oral style with the opening sentences Abenaki writer-storyteller Joseph Bruchac uses in his retelling of a tale of the neighboring Passamaquoddy, "The Girl and the Chenoo":

> *Long ago, there was a girl whose older brothers were hunters. When they went on their hunting trips far into the forest, she would sometimes go with them. Because she was always ready to hear their stories, they called her Little Listener and were happy to have her along. As she was the youngest, Little Listener was usually the one chosen to stay behind and take care of their camp.*

While we can see that Bruchac's written narrative is a bit more polished, he still maintains the qualities of an oral tale by quickly establishing the time, setting, and main character of the story and then moving right into the action. Very few words are wasted on physical descriptions or on creating a context for the story. And his tone is respectful without being reverential.

Because all traditional literature has its origins in oral storytelling, it is important to look closely at the language that is used in any tale you evaluate. Does the text read well aloud? What words contribute to the quality Dr. Hearne describes as "robust sound"? Do you notice elements that give the text a flavor of oral storytelling, such as colloquial speech or occasional use of second person or questions? Do you notice a repetition of any catch phrases, such as the three bears' observation "Someone has been sitting in my chair"?

The oral origins of the tale will also dictate aspects of plot and character. Since these tales move along quickly, with little time to establish setting and character motivations, we expect rapid transitions and concentrated action. The text itself might seem choppy and disjointed if the author doesn't use vivid language or establish patterns through repetition. Consider, for example, how "The Three Bears" might read without its patterned language:

> *Three bears decided to go for a walk while their porridge was cooling. While they were gone, a little girl named Goldilocks entered their*

house. She tasted the porridge in the first two bowls and then ate all the porridge in the third one. She sat in the bears' chairs and broke the smallest one. She went upstairs and tried out all the bears' beds. She found the smallest one to be the most comfortable, and she fell asleep on it. She was still sleeping when the bears returned home. They noticed someone had been eating their porridge and sitting in their chairs. Then they went upstairs and noticed someone had been sleeping in their beds, too. The smallest bear cried out, "She's still here!" That woke Goldilocks up and she jumped out the window and ran away. The three bears never saw her again.

Given this basic bare-bones retelling, we can see how much the story depends on the use of repetition and pattern in the language that is used to retell it. In trying to determine the quality of a retelling, it can be helpful to think of the story in terms of its most basic plot outline, as I have done above with "The Three Bears." This will make the reteller's language stand out. How has the author used language to make the retelling engaging and easy to listen to? What descriptive phrases and actions are used to characterize the key players in the story? You will note, for example, that the three bears lose all their distinguishing characteristics when they are no longer described in terms of size or their connections to Goldilocks' response to their individual chairs, beds, and bowls of porridge.

ILLUSTRATIONS

In the past decade we have seen a tremendous increase in the publication of picture-book versions of folktales for children, partly to meet the increasing demands for multicultural literature and partly to meet the increasing demands from artists who use picture books as a means of showcasing their art. It is not unusual, for example, to see more than one picture-book version of the same story published in any given year.

Because traditional literature is by its nature generally devoid of extensive description, these stories are ripe for countless illustrative treatments by artists with distinctive and diverse styles. Four picture-book versions of "Hansel and Gretel" published within a five-year time period, for example, contain remarkably similar texts—all were taken from faithful English translations of the story as it appeared in the Brothers Grimm's 1812 *Children's and Household Tales.* But in the hands of four different illustrators, no two versions look alike.

Austrian artist Lisbeth Zwerger emphasizes the isolation and abandonment of Hansel and Gretel by making the two solitary children the focal point of every illustration. Very little attention is given to background details of any kind, and we often see only their two figures set against a backdrop of somber earth tones that fade into nothingness. Conversely, American artist Susan Jeffers pays great attention to the children's natural surroundings, with leaves, flowers, birds, and other forest creatures in great abundance placed in the foreground of nearly every illustration. Her art suggests that it is human contact, not the forest, that holds danger for the pair.

Another American artist, Paul O. Zelinsky, gives the story a more literal interpretation, with his richly detailed oil paintings that suggest the works of seventeenth-century Dutch genre paintings. His attention to clothing styles and household interiors puts the story into a definite historical context. So, too, do the illustrations by British artist Anthony Browne; however, he places the story a little closer to home by setting it in the late twentieth century: Hansel and Gretel's bleak existence, as they sit around a bare kitchen table, includes a blaring television in the background, and as they lie in bed at night, a bottle of Oil of Olay sits on their stepmother's dresser. Browne's illustrations also add a psychological layer to the story by subtly suggesting that the stepmother and the witch are one and the same.

Personal tastes aside, none of these versions is necessarily superior to the others or a more faithful rendition of the original tale. Each one stands out as distinctive, and happily, there is plenty of room for all of them. By looking at multiple versions of the same tale, we can even sharpen our evaluative skills, as they lead us to think about those elements that are truly original and to consider how well they complement the story.

Complications can arise when an artist attempts to illustrate a story from outside her realm of cultural experience. If the artist has little or no background in a particular area and is unwilling or unable to do thorough research, she is in danger of misinterpreting the story through illustrations, especially if an attempt is made to imitate "native" styles. It is very difficult for an outsider to extract details effectively without an understanding of the overall context from which they come.

In 1995 two markedly different illustrated versions of the same Ethiopian folktale were published as picture books, causing a lively dialogue among critics and librarians that was played out in the pages of *School Library Journal*. The first, Nancy Raines Day's *The Lion's Whiskers: An Ethiopian Folktale* (Scholastic, 1995), won critical praise for artist Ann Grifalconi's striking use of the collage technique in her illustrations. Two letters to the editor in subsequent issues of *School Library Journal*, however, pointed out inaccuracies in the visual presentation of clothing, houses, and physical landscapes. The reviewer responded to these criticisms by pointing out that Grifalconi's abstract illustrations were not meant to reflect reality; rather, they strove to complement the flavor of the story.

The second version, *Pulling the Lion's Tale* (Simon & Schuster, 1995) by Jane Kurtz, featured more realistic illustrations by Floyd Cooper, and these, according to Ethiopian content specialist Gebregeorgis Yohannes, come much closer to accurately depicting the setting and characters. The controversy inspired author Jane Kurtz to write an article for *School Library Journal,* detailing the complex issues that arise when one publishes a folktale from another country as a picture book. Arguing that visual accuracy is just as important as textual integrity, Kurtz goes on to make a plea for informed, responsible choices at every step of the way in a book's creation. She concludes: "Given that most teachers and librarians have no way of knowing whether a story or its illustrations accurately reflect real lives of real people in the world, authors, illustrators, reviewers, editors and art directors all have some talking to do, to one another and to those whose traditions are depicted in the books." Essentially, Kurtz is echoing what editor Phoebe Yeh had pointed out in 1993: that while folktales on the surface seem to offer ready-made multicultural literature, they can be uniquely challenging to the author, illustrator, editor, and critic. Like the author, the illustrator must also approach the work with scholarship and authenticity.

Beyond judging the quality of the illustrations themselves, as you would do with any picture book, think about how well they complement the story. Has the artist tried to give a sense of the place and culture from which the tale comes and, if so, has he or she succeeded? Does the style the artist used blend well with the tone of the story? What details has the artist added to expand characterization or define setting? Does the artist add a personal interpretation to the story through the use of mood or symbols?

COLLECTIONS

In addition to picture-book editions of single tales, many traditional stories are published in collections of stories, which are generally aimed at children ages eight to twelve. While these collections may include occasional illustrations, the emphasis here is on the stories themselves, and there is generally some unifying characteristic that binds them together. They may be stories from a particular nation or ethnic group, for example, such as Lynette Dyer Vuong and Manabu Saito's *The Golden Carp, and Other Tales from Vietnam* (Lothrop, 1993), or they may be stories of a particular type, as in Virginia Hamilton's collection of creation myths, *In the Beginning: Creation Stories from Around the World* (Harcourt, 1988).

DOCUMENTATION OF SOURCES

Even when stories in a collection come from a common cultural source, the reteller generally consults a variety of original source material to pull together a collection of stories. Because this is most often the case, we expect the author to provide documentation and source notes for each individual story included in the collection.

Author Alvin Schwartz sets the standard for this sort of documentation in his collections of folklore aimed at children. Even in his simplest books, such as the beginning reader *In a Dark, Dark Room and Other Scary Stories* (Harper, 1984), he includes source notes entitled

"Where the Stories Come From" that are aimed at the beginning readers themselves. His popular collections of frightening folklore aimed at older children include extensive notes; for the twenty-nine stories included in *Scary Stories to Tell in the Dark* (Harper, 1981), for example, Schwartz provides what Betsy Hearne has referred to as "model source notes." To research and document the stories he retold, he consulted eighty-four print sources and more than a dozen informants (both children and adults who shared their scary stories with him). In his notes for each story he acknowledges the source(s) he used, discusses variants, and tells how he arrived at the final version that appears in his book.

ORGANIZATION

Schwartz also organizes the stories into sections by type: jump stories, ghost stories, scary things, urban legends, and humorous stories. Each section is introduced with a one- or two-sentence description of the story type, and at the end of the book more extensive notes give further background about each of the tale types, including such things as various techniques for telling a jump tale and the current social environment that makes urban legends appealing.

Other compilers have chosen to organize collections by places or cultures of origin, or by subject. When you evaluate a collection of traditional tales, think about how it is organized. Will the organization assist readers who may be looking for just one or two particular tales? Will it invite readers to approach the collected stories as one continuous narrative? Does the author provide a written introduction to the stories in each section that explains how the part is distinctive and how it relates to the collection as a whole? What is the range of tale types within each section, as well as the range of tales in the entire book?

LITERARY FOLKTALES

These tales are not part of traditional literature, but I will mention them here because they are often confused with traditional tales. Rather than originating within a particular culture's oral storytelling tradition, a literary folktale is written by a known author who uses the characteristics we associate with folktales: concentrated action, stock characters, elements of fantasy, and simple themes. Hans Christian Andersen and Oscar Wilde are perhaps the best-known authors of this type of tale; however, many contemporary authors try their hand at this as well. They are often difficult to distinguish from true folktales, so be on the lookout for descriptive phrases, such as "an original tale," in subtitles or flap copy. Also, check the CIP on the copyright page. The Library of Congress assigns the Dewey decimal number 398 to traditional literature, 290 to mythology, and [FIC] or [E] to literary folktales, although it is not always infallible in its classifications.

Poetry, Verse, Rhymes, and Songs

Rhythm, rhyme, and the pleasurable sounds that words can make appeal to children from a very early age. It is no accident that lullabies are sung to soothe babies and nursery rhymes are recited to entertain them. Children of all ages like the sounds of poetry in language. Older children chant rhymes as they play games and jump rope. They revise the lyrics of commercial jingles to amuse their peers and twist names and words to taunt their enemies. They re-create the rhythms and rhymes of popular music to pass the time as they wait for the school bus on chilly mornings. We find an appetite for poetry everywhere we find children.

Yet many children claim to dislike poetry. In all likelihood what they dislike is the study of poetry. Because poetry is defined in part by form and structure, over the years children in school have been forced to think about poems in these terms. Many adults themselves have unpleasant memories of being forced to dissect a poem to analyze its meaning, and they have come to associate this unpleasantness with poetry in general. But poetry need not be picked apart to be understood and appreciated. It speaks to children through sound, images, and ideas.

THE SOUND OF POETRY

Poetry uses words in musical, rhythmic patterns that delight small children even before they understand the meaning of the words. As children get older, they are better able to appreciate the subtleties of poetic form and content, but young children seem to be especially attracted to regular structured patterns, more aptly called *verse*.

Rhyme, the repetition of the same or similar sounds, is an important part of verse and, to some extent, poetry. There are many kinds of rhyme, but when most people use the word, they are generally referring to *end rhyme* only. End rhyme is the regularly occurring echo that is used in a uniform pattern at the conclusions of lines, and it is the hallmark of conventional verse, particularly verse that is aimed at very young children. While it can be pleasing to the ear and may make a poem easier to listen to and remember, it can also lead to a singsongy regularity that deadens the senses. In fact, many believe that end rhyme is such an artificial and unnatural way of using language, in the hands of a lesser poet it can destroy the essence of poetry. Writers can easily become so bound to rhyme that it dictates the word choice, and the words lose their power and meaning. That is the opposite of what a poet strives for.

Many other devices of sound contribute to rhyme in a pleasurable but less obvious way. These include **alliteration** (the repetition of initial consonant sounds), **assonance** (the repetition of vowel sounds), and **consonance** (the repetition of final consonants). Karla Kuskin uses all the above sound devices in her poem "Thistles."

> *Thirty thirsty thistles*
> *Thicketed and green*
> *Growing in a grassy swamp*
> *Purple-topped and lean*
> *Prickly and thistly*
> *Topped by tufts of thorns*
> *Green mean little leaves on them*
> *And tiny purple horns*
> *Briary and brambly*
> *A spiky, spiney bunch of them.*
> *A troop of bright-red birds came by*
> *And had a lovely lunch of them.*

Both poetry and verse have some sort of rhythm, called **meter**. The lengths of a poem's lines and the pattern of stressed and unstressed syllables constitutes its meter. It not only contributes to the way a poem sounds but can also reinforce the poem's meaning. Meter can be used to slow the reader down and give a sense of quiet contemplation or dreaming, or to move us along quickly to communicate such things as playful movement. Note how the

poet Eloise Greenfield uses short lines to reinforce
meaning in this stanza from her poem about a child in
motion:

> *When Lessie runs she runs so fast that*
> *Sometimes she falls down*
> *But she gets right up and brushes her knees*
> *And runs again as fast as she can*
> *Past red houses*
> > *and parked cars*
> > *and bicycles*
> > *and sleeping dogs*
> > *and cartwheeling girls*
> > *and wrestling boys*
> > *and Mr. Taylor's record store*
> *All the way to the corner*
> *To meet her mama*

The two- and three-word lines list the people and
things Lessie passes as she's running, and also give a sense
of her feet pounding on the pavement in her breathless
sprint down the street, until she finally slows down when
she reaches the corner.

Modern poetry has gradually moved away from a
reliance on a strict rhythm and the use of end rhymes.
Poems need not rhyme at all, and **free verse** breaks away
from formal metrical patterns altogether. Arnold Adoff is
one of the best-known children's poets who brings a
modern vision to poetry. His poems often tell a story by
combining strong feeling with action.

I am near the shoulder
>> *of the girl*
>> *in the lead*

and maybe this lead girl
>>> *looks*
>>>> *back*
for a second
to see if i am still
>> *on her shoulder*

then my eyes
tell her
>> *good*
>> *bye*

In Adoff's poems, the placement of the words on the page is almost like a road map, giving readers guidance as to how they should read the poems aloud.

THE IMAGES OF POETRY

Since poems are compact, there can be no wasted words. The poet carefully chooses precise, exact words to evoke the desired mood or feeling, or to surprise the reader with an unexpected—but perfect—comparison. Poetry uses **metaphor**, bringing unrelated things together to point out similarities or differences. Pay close attention to the way Gwendolyn Brooks uses words to create images and feelings in "Cynthia in the Snow" from her book *Bronzeville Boys and Girls* (Harper, 1956):

> *It SUSHES.*
> *It hushes*
> *The loudness in the road.*
> *It flitter-twitters,*
> *And laughs away from me.*
> *It laughs a lovely whiteness,*
> *And whitely whirs away,*
> *To be*
> *Some otherwhere,*
> *Still white as milk or shirts.*
> *So beautiful it hurts.*

Brooks uses imagery to appeal to the senses of hearing, sight, and touch, making us feel as though we are right in the midst of a snow flurry. Her playful use of words — "laughs away from me," "whitely" and "otherwhere" — is original and inventive, and yet can be immediately understood. On a metaphorical level, Brooks writes about snow as if it were a person, another child perhaps, teasing and enticing Cynthia as a playmate might do.

THE IDEAS OF POETRY

Like "Cynthia in the Snow," good children's poetry gives fresh vision to common things and experiences. It can appeal to the intellect, as well as the emotions, as it extends and enriches meaning in everyday life. In looking at children's poetry on an intellectual level, we need to

keep in mind the typical interests and concerns of childhood: relationships with friends and family, the outdoors,
daily routines, play, animals, and ordinary everyday things
such as safety pins or socks—these are pieces of the child's
world. We can find them all in good poetry for children.

When we evaluate children's poetry, we need to consider the quality of the poetry itself by thinking about how
it sounds, what it says, and how it says it. Read poetry
aloud. A good poem sounds natural, even if it rhymes.
Look at the words that have been used in composing the
poem. Do they seem unchangeable? What kinds of specific and implied comparisons has the poet made? How
has imagery been used? Think about the idea presented in
the poem. Does it show a fresh view of something with
which a child is likely to be familiar? Does it appeal to the
mind through the senses? Does it leave a lingering image
in the mind of the reader?

In addition to thinking about the quality of the poetry
itself, we also need to consider the manner in which it is
presented in a book. Poetry published for children exists in
great quantity and variety. We find books that appeal to all
ages, from infancy up through the teen years. There are
anthologies of classic poems, some of which were written
specifically for children and some of which were written for
adults but can be enjoyed by children. There are collections
of poems by individual poets. There are single poems that
are illustrated and published as individual picture books, as
well as picture-book texts written in verse. And there are
collections of songs published in anthologies, in addition to
single songs published in picture-book editions. Because

poetry, rhymes, and verse appeal to a broad range of ages, we need to think in terms of audience when we evaluate individual volumes of poetry. Let's take a look at some of these categories, beginning with rhymes for the very youngest.

NURSERY RHYMES

Nursery rhymes recited to children and handed down through generations have come to be associated with the appropriately fanciful name Mother Goose. In their authoritative work on the subject, *The Oxford Dictionary of Nursery Rhymes* (Oxford, 1951), folklore scholars Peter and Iona Opie remark that while many scholarly studies have attempted to analyze the symbolic and historical nature of the rhymes, these interpretations are largely speculative. The rhymes themselves have survived not because of a great underlying meaning—indeed, many of them make little sense at all—but because of their sound: "[T]hese trivial verses have endured where newer and more ambitious compositions have become dated and forgotten. They have endured for nine or ten generations, sometimes for considerably more, and scarcely altered in their journey."

While surviving as oral literature for generations, the rhymes began to be published in books especially created for children in the early eighteenth century. They are among the earliest children's books published in both England and the United States. For the most part the rhymes they contain are familiar to English-speaking children today: "Baa Baa Black Sheep," "Little Jack Horner," and "This Little Pig Went to Market" among them.

The rhymes themselves don't change, but the illustrations do. Each year new editions of Mother Goose nursery rhymes are added to the selection of contemporary children's books. Illustrations offer new interpretations or fresh presentations of familiar characters. Lucy Cousins' *The Little Dog Laughed, and Other Nursery Rhymes* (Dutton, 1989) has a distinctly modern feel with the artist's use of bold flat colors and abstract shapes outlined with thick black lines. Her inclusion of brown-skinned characters enhances its contemporary spirit. On the opposite end of the scale, illustrator Faith Jaques purposely sets the rhymes in the eighteenth century in Zena Sutherland's *The Orchard Book of Nursery Rhymes* (Orchard, 1990). Her interpretation, coupled with the author's detailed source notes, stresses the historical nature of the rhymes. Arnold Lobel also sets his illustrations in an earlier time period in *The Random House Book of Mother Goose: A Treasury of 306 Timeless Nursery Rhymes* (Random House, 1986) but his light touches bring out the humor and playfulness in the rhymes.

How do we evaluate these collections? Look at the illustrations to determine what they add to the rhymes. What scenes did the illustrator choose to show? Due to the harsh and violent nature of many of the rhymes, literal interpretations will not always work. We may enjoy the image of the baby rocking in his cradle in a treetop, but few parents will want to share a picture that shows his unfortunate descent when the bough breaks. Conversely, every child wants to see Jack and Jill falling down the hill and Humpty Dumpty falling off the wall. A skilled and thoughtful illustrator takes the sensibilities of small children and their parents into consideration.

Look at the selection of rhymes included in the collection. Which rhymes have been included? Is it a fairly comprehensive collection, or is it selective? Are most of the rhymes familiar ones, such as "Little Miss Muffet" and "Little Boy Blue"? Adults who are looking for collections of nursery rhymes to share with their children generally want to find the ones they remember from childhood. Less familiar rhymes may be included, but they shouldn't outnumber the common rhymes unless that is the point of the book, as it is in the Opies' *Tail Feathers from Mother Goose* (Little, Brown, 1988), a collection of obscure nursery rhymes from various sources housed in the Opie archive. How does the author provide access to the rhymes? Is there an alphabetical index by title or by first line (often one and the same in nursery rhymes)? If someone were looking for the complete version of "London Bridge Is Falling Down," for example, could it be easily found in the collection?

Since most nursery rhymes are short, they don't all lend themselves to single-rhyme editions of picture books; however, some do. James Marshall has given us a hilarious interpretation of the rhyme *Old Mother Hubbard and Her Wonderful Dog* (Farrar, 1991) by exaggerating the absurdities in the rhyme itself. Bruce McMillan gave us a completely new vision of Sarah Josepha Hale's familiar nursery rhyme *Mary Had a Little Lamb* (Scholastic, 1990), by illustrating it with photographs of an African-American girl wearing glasses and yellow overalls.

HUMOROUS POETRY AND LIGHT VERSE

Nursery rhymes adhere to strict patterns of rhythm and rhyme and would be strictly classified as *verse* rather than as poetry. Although the terms "poetry" and "verse" are often used interchangeably, it is fairly easy to draw distinctions between the two, and it's helpful to do so in order to speak and write more precisely. Both poetry and verse use patterned language to condense thoughts and ideas into a structured form. Verse, however, rarely strays from its regular structure; poetry often does. Verse generally deals in lighter subjects and presents ideas as an open-and-shut case, but poetry opens a window onto a thought or experience through use of metaphor and imagery.

When verse uses trite ideas and hackneyed language, it becomes *doggerel,* an inferior form best reserved for greeting cards. Verse succeeds on a grand scale, however, when it draws humor from wild incongruity or plants verbal surprises within a rigid structure. The **nonsense verse** of the nineteenth-century writers Edward Lear and Lewis Carroll continues to delight today's children with its daft impossibilities. There is something about outrageous absurdity bound up in a tight, predictable structure that elementary-school-aged children find fall-down-on-the-floor funny. Shel Silverstein is a master at this kind of writing, and his collections *Where the Sidewalk Ends* (Harper, 1974), *A Light in the Attic* (Harper, 1981) and *Falling Up* (Harper, 1996), are among the best-selling children's hardcover trade books of all time. The zany nonsense verses of Ogden Nash, John Ciardi, and Jack Prelutsky are also extremely popular with children.

Humor in general holds great appeal, from the classic nonsense of Edward Lear to the more subtle uses of humor we see in light verse and poetry. It can open a door into poetry for children and draw them into a vision that offers new insight and meaning. Note, for example, how X. J. Kennedy uses humor to give children a fresh perspective on an ordinary object:

Lighting a Fire
One quick scratch
Of a kitchen match
And giant flames unzip!

How do they store
So huge a roar
In such a tiny tip?

Many writers of children's poetry excel at using wit and humor to stir children's interest and imaginations. Rather than telling children what is funny, these poets are able to see the humor and incongruities in life that children themselves may notice and wonder about. Other than poets and children, for instance, how many people stop to reflect on what happens when you strike a match?

Nonsense verse and humorous poetry differ, to some extent, in form and content, but both offer the reader surprises that inspire laughter. In verse these surprises are generally dependent on the tension between words and structure. Poetry uses this tension as well, but also adds an intangible element in the metaphorical tension of ideas that lie under the surface of the poem. X. J. Kennedy does not explicitly compare a kitchen match to a lion, for example, but he suggests it with his choice of the word "roar." As you evaluate humorous verse and poetry, think about the sources of its humor. Does it come from the description of things, people, and places engaged in absurd actions? Or does it come from a more subtle juxtaposition of unlike things or ideas? How does the structure enhance its surprising and pleasurable aspects? Would you look forward to reading the poems aloud to children? Above all, poems are meant to be read aloud— that's often the best test of a poem.

POETRY COLLECTIONS

SINGLE POETS

Children's poems are generally published in collections that may contain anywhere from a dozen to a hundred or more poems. Collections of poems by a single children's poet are quite common, in which case authorship alone may be the unifying factor. Some poets issue volumes of poetry on a common theme. Arnold Adoff, for example, has issued separate volumes of poetry on subjects such as sports, chocolate, and identity. Others issue volumes limited to a certain form. Valerie Worth is known for her collections of very short poems about small things, and Gary Soto has gathered together a verbal celebration of community in his *Neighborhood Odes* (Harcourt, 1992). Paul Fleischman was awarded the Newbery Medal in 1989 for *Joyful Noise: Poems for Two Voices* (Zolotow/Harper, 1988), a volume of poems that echo the pattern of classical Greek odes in that they are written to be read aloud by two voices.

ANTHOLOGIES

Anthologies pull together the works of many poets. There is an art to collecting and anthologizing poetry that calls for a closer look on the part of the critic. Skillful anthologists pull together poems on a common theme or topic and organize them in an arrangement that makes them aesthetically and intellectually satisfying.

Anthologies of poetry collected by William Cole are exemplary in their organization, as can been seen in the contents page from *A Book of Nature Poems* (Viking, 1969):

O Feel the Gentle Air: Spring and Blossoming

Green Thoughts in a Green Shade: Flowers and Gardens

Of Neptune's Empire Let Us Sing: Rivers, Lakes and the Sea

A Blaze of Noons: Summer's Sweetness

Wait for the Moon to Rise: Night, Stars and the Moon

Season of the Mists and Mellow Fruitfulness: Autumn and Harvest

About the Woodlands I Will Go: Trees and the Woods

The Wind Stood Up and Gave a Shout: Wind, Rain and
   Storm

When Icicles Hang by the Wall: Snow and Winter

To Stand and Stare: Various Celebrations of Nature's
   Miracles

Just by looking at the contents page we can see the beauty and the order of Coles' anthology, which is arranged not only by subject (bodies of water, astronomical entities, etc.) but also by the cycle of seasons. Like all good anthologies, this one also includes indices that give access by the names of poets included, as well as titles and first lines of the poems.

Lee Bennett Hopkins, Nancy Larrick, Myra Cohn Livingston, and Lilian Moore are outstanding anthologists of poetry for young readers. Their topical anthologies cover subjects such as animals, family and friends, holidays, science, nature, city life, and bedtime. Both Hopkins and Moore have compiled collections aimed at particular age groups as well. For *Sunflakes: Poems for Children* (Clarion, 1992) Moore selected seventy-five outstanding poems for very young children, dealing with high-interest topics such as bugs, puddles, potato chips, and the marvels of breathing on windowpanes in winter. Lee Bennett Hopkins has selected thirty-seven poems that are accessible to beginning readers in *Surprises* (Zolotow/ Harper, 1984), which includes poets such as Langston Hughes and Christina Rossetti.

There are numerous anthologies of poetry collected for older children along similar lines. One of the most remarkable skills of good anthologists for this age level,

however, is an ability to cull from works originally published for adults and select those poems that will speak
to the young as well. This skill combines a thorough knowledge of poetry with a thorough knowledge of children
and young teenagers. Ruth Gordon, Paul Janeczko, and
Naomi Shihab Nye compile stunning anthologies based
on poetry from a wide range of times, places, and experiences. These anthologies not only provide young readers
with collections of fine poetry, they also give them a
sense of being connected as individuals to universal human
emotions.

Look at the range of poems and poets included in any
anthology. Are there new poems as well as older ones?
Are the poems selected from a broad range of cultures?
Do they have a common theme or subject? How are they
arranged? How does the anthologist provide access with
various types of indices? In the best anthologies the compiler's enthusiasm for poetry is apparent through the
careful selections and arrangements she has made.

SONGS

One might argue that songs were meant to be sung, not
written down; but as long as human memories remain fal-
lible, there will be songs committed to the pages of books.
As they appear in trade books, songs share many features
in common with poetry; unlike most poetry, however, they
appeared at first in some form other than writing.

Songbooks for children typically include musical notation as an accompaniment to the text. If the lyrics to a

single song are written out in story form as the text of a picture book, the musical notation may appear at the end of the book. The quality of the notation should be evaluated as carefully as text and illustrations. Is the arrangement simple enough to be accessible to children? Is it in a singable key? Is the notation legible and easy to read? Does it include all the song's verses, and have they been conveniently placed so that it is possible to follow along if one is playing or singing the song aloud?

John Langstaff is noted for his compilations of British and American folk songs and ballads, such as *Hi! Ho! The Rattling Bog, and Other Folk Songs for Group Singing* (Harcourt, 1969). The lyrics to each of these songs drawn from many sources are accompanied by their musical notation, as well as a brief note that places the song in a historical context. Cheryl Warren Mattox uses a similar approach in her unusual collection *Shake It to the One That You Love the Best: Play Songs and Lullabies from Black Musical Traditions* (Warren-Mattox, 1990). In both of these volumes the added background research done by the authors gives added meaning to familiar songs.

Other books of song are highly visual. Ashley Bryan is known for the captivating paintings he creates to interpret songs in his books, such as *All Night, All Day: A Child's First Book of African-American Spirituals* (Atheneum, 1991). Picture-book editions of single songs are less common but not unknown. Feodor Rojankovsky's illustrations for Langstaff's *Frog Went A-Courtin'* (Harcourt, 1955) won the Caldecott Medal in 1956. The text in this case was a retelling of the 400-year-old Scottish ballad.

A critical approach to books of song requires consideration of some of the standards we use in evaluating poetry as we look at the presentation of language in a structured pattern. It also requires the sort of critical attention we give to folklore, as we must think about source notes, organization, and in some cases retelling. Overall we need to ask whether or not one art form (music) has made a successful transition to another (art and literature).

Picture Books

Books for young children combine words with illustrations to tell a story. They are meant to be read aloud while children view the illustrations. Picture books present a special challenge to the critic because they require evaluation of art, text, and how the two work together to create a unique art form. In evaluating picture books, it is also useful for the critic to have an understanding of common interests and cognitive abilities of young children at different stages in their development.

Picture books as we know them today are a fairly recent invention. Children's books that combined short text and illustrations to tell a story were developed by European artists and printers in the mid-nineteenth century; however, it was not until 1928 that the modern American picture book was born with the publication of Wanda Gág's *Millions of Cats* (Coward-McCann). While earlier efforts set story and pictures side by side, Gág was the first to take art beyond conventional illustration: Her pictures helped to tell the story by using negative space to indicate the passage of time, varied page layouts, and illustrations that broke out of their frames to extend across two pages. These innovations were immediately imitated and refined by other artists creating books for young children, and very soon they were considered conventions of the art itself.

In 1938, ten years after the publication of *Millions of Cats*, the Randolph Caldecott Medal was established to recognize excellence in picture-book art. The decades that followed are often thought of as a "Golden Age" of picture books, as this new art form attracted the talents of many gifted artists working in the variety of styles that have flourished in twentieth-century art.

During these years, books with color illustrations often required the artist to go through the painstaking process of preseparating colors by hand for offset printing. An artist was allowed to work with one, two, three, or four colors, depending on the publisher's budget (the more colors, the more expensive the production). In three-color art, for instance, an artist might choose to use black, blue, and yellow and would then preseparate the art by first preparing the portions of the picture that were black (generally referred to as a *keyplate*), then painting on separate sheets called *overlays* the portions that were blue and the portions that were yellow, so that the finished art would actually be the three sheets, layered one on top of another. This technique required commitment, skill, and patience

on the part of the artist, in addition to a thorough understanding of color and an ability to visualize the whole by
analyzing its parts (what proportions of blue and yellow
would create the exact shade of green needed?). In spite
of such constraints (or perhaps because of them), we saw
many creative approaches to illustration in black and
white or with one or two colors due to the efforts of artists
who put their hearts and souls into children's book art.

Changes in technology in the mid-1980s, however, had
an enormous impact on book production, especially in the
area of picture books. Advances such as high-speed
presses, computer technology, and scanning devices not
only allowed for accurate reproduction of full-color art,
but also accomplished it at a lower cost. These changes
encouraged the entry of many new fine artists into the
field, employing a great variety of techniques and styles.
Children's book art expert Dilys Evans has characterized
this as a visual renaissance in which "full-color printing
has reached a new plateau of high performance." Even the
slightest, most pedestrian story is given the level of art
production that was formerly reserved for established,
highly regarded book creators such as Ludwig Bemelmans,
Maurice Sendak, and Marcia Brown.

In the midst of this ever-changing world of picture
books, perhaps the factor that remains most constant is
the children themselves. Young children may enjoy being
dazzled by the latest bold venture in picture-book art, but
at the same time they may ask to return again and again to
the familiar comforts of *Goodnight Moon.* Just what is it
about this book that has ensured its success for the last

fifty years? It scores high marks in all the areas that matter when it comes to picture books: 1) outstanding text; 2) excellent illustrations; and 3) successful integration of the two. In addition, it holds enormous appeal for young children, whose obvious pleasure is then transferred to adults who share the book with them. But of course, the child's chance at experiencing any picture book as a whole is completely dependent on someone who is willing and able to read the text aloud. Because picture books function best as a shared experience between a fluent reader and a pre-reader, generally an adult and a young child, in order for a picture book to find true success, it must be good enough to spark this symbiotic relationship.

While all these factors work together to create an aesthetic whole, the critic must break the picture book down into its individual parts in order to evaluate how its components fit together. In this chapter we will look at the picture book in terms of words, pictures, and how the two work together.

TEXT

Anyone who has ever read picture books aloud to children knows just how important the words that make up the text are. Since most picture books are thirty-two pages in length, and since most of those pages are covered with illustrations, their texts are necessarily short. There is another reason for the economical use of words: Preschoolers simply have limits as to what they can and will take in. Lengthy descriptions and sophisticated abstractions are unnecessary and pointless. In picture books, as in poetry, every word counts. But beyond telling a compelling story in few words, a good picture-book text has a distinctive *structure* based on familiar patterns. In order to evaluate picture books, we must ask ourselves not only "What is this story about?" but also "How is this story told?" And when it comes to studying the structural elements of a successful picture-book text, we can find no better model than the "Laureate of the Nursery," Margaret Wise Brown.

STRUCTURE

Not too long after Wanda Gág launched American picture books with the publication of *Millions of Cats*, writer Margaret Wise Brown entered the scene. As a teacher of two- to five-year-olds in the Bank Street School during the mid-1930s, Brown was a keen observer of the developmental behavior of her young charges. She was also greatly influenced by the groundbreaking work of her mentor, Lucy Sprague Mitchell, who asserted that when it came to words, rhythm and sound quality were more important to young children than meaning. It was during this time that Brown began to write her picture books.

PATTERNED LANGUAGE

Rhythm and sound are the hallmarks of Brown's picture-book texts. She accomplishes this by building a pattern with words that are rooted in a young child's experience and understanding of the world. In Brown's "Noisy Books," for example, routines in the everyday world are made extraordinary as children are asked to consider them from the perspective of a little dog named Muffin, who experiences the world by hearing it:

> *And then there was a rattle of dishes. That*
> *meant lunch.*
> > *What kind of noise did lunch make?*
>
> *They had celery for lunch*
> > *Could Muffin hear that?*
> *And soup*
> > *Could Muffin hear that?*
> *And raw carrots*
> > *and steak*
> > > *and spinach*
> > *Could Muffin hear that?*
>
> *And some very quiet custard for dessert*

All the elements of patterned language that contribute to the success of picture-book texts for young children can be found in the above-quoted passage from *The Indoor Noisy Book* (Harper, 1942). They are:

RHYTHM

Note the variation in line lengths, which, as in poetry, gives the reader clues as to how to read the words. But even if these lines were written out as paragraphs, they would still maintain most of their rhythm due to Brown's choice of words: "rattle of dishes" sounds very much like what it describes, and the succession of three trochees, "very quiet custard," naturally causes readers to slow down and speak in softer tones. The sentence "That meant lunch." packs a punch with its three accented beats that grab and hold the listener's attention. It has exactly the same familiar rhythm as the parental attention grabber "I said no." In fact, because they are often inexperienced listeners, young children's attention wanders easily. Brown places this sort of rhythmic hook at regular intervals to draw them back.

RHYME

While rhyme in *The Indoor Noisy Book* is not obvious as it is in many other picture books, it is in fact there in the pleasing repetition of sounds and sentences that appear throughout the story. In addition to making a text easier for children to listen to, rhyme also enhances the predictability of a story. When young children listen to a rhyming story, they can generally supply the last word in a couplet or a quatrain, provided the subject is within the realm of their experience.

REPETITION

Brown skillfully alternates repeated lines with the introduction of words or concepts that may be new to children. By doing so she is using a familiar, expected pattern to make children feel comfortable and ready to face the unfamiliar and unexpected. Once she has set up the pattern with "Could Muffin hear that?" for example, as soon as children hear the words "raw carrots and steak and spinach," they begin to think about the sounds each of these foods makes. And once they have entered this realm of creative thinking, they are more than ready to face the imaginative challenge of "very quiet custard."

QUESTIONS

The question-answer mode is a language pattern very familiar to young children. The "Noisy Books" are filled with questions that inspire children to think about what sorts of sounds Muffin is hearing and the sources of various sounds he hears. In the context of picture-book texts, questions serve a couple of different purposes. Since they are generally read with a different intonation, they add variety to the sound and rhythm of the text. They can also serve as hooks that will pull in wandering minds and help to keep the audience's attention focused. In addition, they also directly involve the child in the story, something that not only makes a story more interesting for everyone but also enhances the self-concept of the child. With young children, there is no such thing as a rhetorical question: If the text asks a question, you will probably get answers. The answers to some questions may be obvious to some children: "Is this red?" "Noooo! It's blue!" Others, such as "What kind of noise did lunch make?" require creative thinking and may lead to several possible answers. Lastly, questions help the adult reader silently assess the level of understanding and appreciation on the part of the child audience.

The pleasing sound of patterned language is especially effective in picture books aimed at two- and three-year-olds. It functions almost like a net to catch and hold the young listeners' attention. It should not, however, overwhelm the story. The most successful uses of patterned language reveal themselves when the text is read aloud. Even when preschoolers become more experienced listeners and are able to rely more on meaning, elements of patterned language can greatly enrich stories aimed at three- and four-year-olds, since children at this age level generally enjoy word play a great deal.

PREDICTABILITY

As children gain experience with listening to stories, they begin to develop an understanding that stories follow a regular sequence. This idea can be reinforced with repeated rereadings of the same story (generally at the child's request), as children become so familiar with the story that they can easily predict what will happen next. Sometimes writers of picture books build predictability right into the text with repeated actions or phrases or by using the same sentence structure over and over again. Like patterned language, predictable structures make stories easier for children to listen to and comprehend. They also allow authors to introduce more surprising or unusual elements successfully within a carefully constructed familiar context. The contrast between the predictable and the surprising elements often delights adults as well as children.

In the classic picture book *The Runaway Bunny* (Harper, 1942) Margaret Wise Brown used predictability in two ways: action and sentence structure. In this story of a small bunny trying to establish a separate identity from his mother while at the same time testing her unconditional love, each action on the bunny's part elicits a predictable reaction on the mother's part:

> *"If you run after me," said the little bunny,*
> *"I will become a fish in a trout stream*
> *and I will swim away from you."*
>
> *"If you become a fish in a trout stream," said his mother,*
> *"I will become a fisherman and I will fish for you."*
>
> *"If you become a fisherman," said the little bunny,*
> *"I will become a rock on the mountain, high above you."*
>
> *"If you become a rock on the mountain high above me,"*
> *said his mother, "I will be a mountain climber,*
> *and I will climb to where you are."*

Children hearing this text soon pick up on the pattern of the bunny vowing to turn into someone or something else, while his mother responds by placing herself imaginatively in the same context so she can find him. This comforting predictability is also reinforced in Brown's repetition of the same sentence structure: "If you . . . I will . . ." The pleasantly surprising aspects of the bunny's playful threats and his mother's clever responses to them balance perfectly with the predictable elements, so that the text seems fresh, even after multiple readings.

PACE

While patterned language and predictability are especially important in books for two- and three-year-olds, pace is an important feature in picture books for all age levels. The best writing we find in picture-book texts takes advantage of this unique art form by acknowledging what has been called "the drama of turning the page."

Margaret Wise Brown was so skilled at pacing picture-book texts that she could actually put a great deal of description into her books and still hold the attention of young listeners. To accomplish this, she broke her text up into meaningful segments, filled with words and images that appeal to children's senses, and used the drama of turning the page to heighten tension. Her book *The Little Island* (Doubleday, 1946, written under the pseudonym Golden MacDonald), for example, deals with an encounter between a kitten, who comes to a small island with people on a picnic, and the island itself. The first ten pages of text, however, are devoted to a description of the island before the kitten arrives. There are five pages of text dealing with a conversation between the kitten and the island and, after the kitten leaves, five more pages of description of the island by itself again. Notice how the text is broken into segments to create an appropriately undulating pace.

Then one day
all the lobsters crawled in from the sea
and hid under the rocks and ledges
of the island to shed their shells
and let their new ones grow hard and strong
in hiding places in the dark.
(turn page)
And the seals came barking from the north
to lie on the sunny rocks
and raise their baby seals.
(turn page)
And the kingfishers came from the South
to build nests.
(turn page)
And the gulls laid their eggs
on the rocky ledges.
(turn page)
And wild strawberries turned red.
Summer had come to the little Island.

Each page segment describes a simple action of one of the natural inhabitants of the island. The author could just as easily have put the seals, kingfishers, gulls, and wild strawberries into one page segment, but instead she took her time, drawing the description out in separate segments over four double spreads. This has the effect of giving young listeners a sense of natural activity amidst the soothing peacefulness of the island.

Due to the the manner in which books are manufactured, the number of pages in any hardcover book is always divisible by eight. Most picture books are thirty-two pages long, though we occasionally see picture books that are forty or forty-eight pages. The writer must work within these confines. In the standard thirty-two-page book, there will generally be fourteen or fifteen segments of text. Each of these segments is rather like a chapter in a novel: Something must happen to move the story along or to add to the overall mood of the book. If too much happens in one segment, however, it can throw off the pace of the story. Who hasn't had the experience of reading aloud to a young child who tires of a particular page before all the text has been read? This may be an indication of poor pacing. For that matter, who hasn't had the experience of reading a picture book silently to oneself and feeling a strong urge to turn the page before reaching the end of the segment of text? That is definitely an indication of poor pacing! If the text doesn't hold *your* attention, how do you expect it to hold the attention of a small child?

Think of this when you evaluate picture books. Do the pages seem to turn in the right places? Does the text flow naturally when you read it aloud? How does it sound? Do you notice elements of patterned language? Are there sentence or plot structures that make the story predictable?

ILLUSTRATIONS

Just as writers use sounds, rhythm, and words to express meaning, artists use line, shape, texture, color, and value. These are called *visual elements*. Artists must make decisions about *composition,* or how to arrange the elements on each page. They must determine which *medium* will be most effective for their work and which *style* to use. They take all these factors into consideration in addition to thinking of the story as a sequence of pictures.

VISUAL ELEMENTS

Visual elements are the components an artist uses in creating a picture: line, shape, texture, color, and value. Most or all of these elements are combined into any one picture; however, oftentimes one element will dominate an artist's work.

LINE

There are only two types of line in art and in nature: straight and curved. These lines may be thick or thin, long or short. They can move in three possible directions: horizontal, vertical, or oblique (at a slant). Artists use directional lines for different effects. When horizontal lines dominate, they give a sense of orderly action that moves from left to right. Dominant vertical lines make a picture look still and static, giving it the photographic effect of a moment captured in time. Oblique lines suggest spontaneous action and excitement, such as that of a person rolling down a hill. Artists use line to guide the viewer's eye across the page. They may also use line to point subtly to the objects in a picture that they want the viewer to look at.

SHAPE

A two-dimensional pattern that is a clear representation of an object (realism); a distorted but still recognizable object (abstraction); or a shape that's an unrecognizable object (nonobjective). Shapes fall into two broad categories: curved or angular. Curved shapes are used to represent objects in nature (people, animals, foliage, the moon, etc.), while angular (especially rectangular) shapes represent artificial, man-made objects (buildings, boxes, trains, books, etc.). Artists may use curved shapes for man-made objects for a desired purpose. For example, Virginia Lee Burton used curved lines to paint the house in *The Little House* (Houghton, 1943), to characterize it as human and to make it look out of place in an urban environment.

TEXTURE

The nature of the surface of shapes in a picture. Texture is best determined by the sense of touch; however, artists can communicate three types of texture visually: smooth (hard), rough, and soft, with the medium used to create a picture (oils, pastels, pencil, etc.) or the medium that receives it (textured paper, wood, etc.). Because texture appeals to our tactile sense, it can be used to give a strong sensual feeling to artwork.

COLOR

We can speak about color in terms of its *hue* (the name by which we distinguish it, such as "red" or "blue"), its *value* (darkness or lightness of any hue, "dark red" or "light blue"), and *chroma* (brightness or intensity). *Achromatic colors* are the shades of gray from white to black, and *monochromatic colors* are the various values of one color. *Primary* colors (red, yellow, and blue) can be mixed with each other to produce *secondary* colors (orange, green, and purple). Together they are divided into two groups: *complementary* colors are two opposing hues, such as red and green or blue and orange, while *analogous* colors are two related hues, such as red and orange or green and yellow. In addition, people often speak of colors as *warm* (red, yellow, orange) or *cool* (blue, green).

VALUE

The lightness or darkness of any color. A hue is mixed with black to give it a darker value and with white (or water) to give it a lighter value. Value is used in black-and-white illustrations to give a sense of depth and volume. In color artwork it can be used to project a mood or to represent the passage of time. When color artwork shows no variation in value, we describe it as flat.

COMPOSITION

An artist must carefully plan how to arrange the visual elements on a page to create the desired mood or effect. This is rarely done without a lot of thought. In fact, if you look carefully at the composition of an illustration, you can generally see several *design principles* at work. While it it entirely possible for an artist to apply any one of the following design principles to all the visual elements in a single picture, it is not necessary for him to do so.

DOMINANCE

Gives a sense of order by drawing the eye to certain reference points in a picture. If there are several shapes in a picture, one will dominate. If there are many colors, one will be more important. Artists create dominance by:

1) Making more of something. If an artist wants a rough texture to dominate, for example, he will make more of the surfaces appear to be rough.

2) Making something larger. To make a particular shape stand out in a picture, an artist can make it appear a lot bigger than the other shapes.

3) Making something brighter. Even a small shape will stand out as dominant if it's more brightly colored than the shapes around it.

4) Giving something more value contrast. Darker objects stand out among light and lighter objects stand out among dark.

BALANCE

Gives a sense of comfort by making one part of the picture equal the other. A *formal* or *symmetrical* balance is one with an even distribution of shapes that would produce a mirrorlike image if the picture were vertically divided into two halves. An *informal* or *asymmetrical* balance results from an irregular distribution of shapes—for example, a large shape placed closer to the center of a picture balances a small shape placed closer to the edge. Colors can also be balanced visually: smaller areas of bright color balance with larger areas of weaker ones.

CONTRAST

Adds excitement to a picture by making an abrupt change in a visual element. An artist may contrast thin lines with thick lines, for example, or an angular shape with a rounded one.

GRADATION

Adds familiarity by reflecting the sorts of gradual change we see in everyday life. A gradation in color shows the gradual change from one color to another, as we see in nature when the sun sets. Gradation in size can give the illusion of depth. Gradation in shape reflects growth and movement.

ALTERNATION

Establishes a regular pattern by alternating between two or more types of the same element—for example, two thin lines alternating repeatedly with a thick line. In picture books we see this technique used most often in decorative borders. It is also used as pattern in depicting things such as wallpaper, curtains, or clothing. Because it consists of a regular repeated pattern, a lot of alternation inspires boredom; however, used judiciously, it can have a striking effect.

VARIATION

Makes an overall composition more complex and engaging by changing elements in line, texture, shape, color, and value.

HARMONY

Gives a feeling of subtle change and continuity by repeating any of the visual elements with only a slight variation. Harmony can be used to slow down the pace without becoming static or boring.

UNITY

Makes the pieces of a picture fit together as a whole so that any smaller part of a picture looks like the rest of it. One way to achieve unity is to repeat or echo one element in another part of the picture.

The artistic elements and principles of design work together to express meaning in picture-book illustrations. This may range from a simple representation of characters and action in a story to a deeper psychological interpretation of meaning conveyed through mood and emotions. A critical look at any picture's components and how they are related will help you to think about an artist's intent. It will add depth to your evaluation of a picture book. Many reviewers focus on *what* happens in a picture book without paying much attention to *how* it happens. But if you understand the elements and the principles of design, you can begin to think more critically about the art in picture books, and you can articulate your observations.

When you look at an illustration, think about the elements and how they are used. What do you notice about the use of line? Does a certain type of line dominate? What effect does this have? Why did the artist strive for this effect? What do you notice about shapes? Are they mostly rounded or are they angular? Does one shape dominate a picture? Why do you think the artist wants to draw your attention to this shape? How is texture used? Does it give a distinctive feeling to the scene? What colors are used? Are they warm or cool? Do they express particular emotions, such as anger (red) or serenity (blue)? How are colors balanced in the picture?

As you turn the pages of a picture book, think about the pictures as they relate to each other. Do you notice continuity or variation in the use of elements? How does this reflect the mood or the action in the story? Do the pictures follow a logical or predictable sequence? Is there a natural movement from one page to the next? Is there an overall sense of unity or harmony in the illustrations?

Finally, think about the illustrations as they fit into the book as a whole. How do they relate to the story? Do they

complement, extend, or highlight the text? Do they provide crucial details that are not present in the text but add
something to the story? Do they clarify in such a way that
they take the story beyond its words?

I will demonstrate how this sort of evaluation works by
using a book that is familiar to most everyone, *Goodnight
Moon* (Harper, 1947) written by Margaret Wise Brown
and illustrated by Clement Hurd. On the surface it
appears to be a simple bedtime story, and yet the fact that
it has persisted as a favorite book among several generations of young children suggests that there is more to it. In
terms of its writing, it has all the important features mentioned earlier in the discussion of text: patterned language, predictability, and a perfect pace. Add to that
Clement Hurd's magnificent illustrations, and the whole is
greater than the sum of its parts. But what exactly is it
about the illustrations that makes them outstanding? Or
are they outstanding? Today, amidst the eye-catching new
picture books on the "plateau of high performance," the
illustrations in *Goodnight Moon* seem to be rather plain
and humble. But the elements and design principles have
not changed: good art is good art, no matter the era. Let's
apply our understanding of visual elements and composition to Hurd's well-loved and familiar pictures to see what
they'll reveal.

First, consider the challenge Hurd faced in illustrating
the text of *Goodnight Moon.* Superficially, the entire story
is set in the same bedroom and consists of a list of objects
present in the room. But Hurd understood the text on a
deeper psychological level and used his understanding to

convey meaning through the illustrations. In a study of the psychology inherent in Margaret Wise Brown's picture-book texts, Dr. Timothy M. Rivinus and Lisa Audet point out that the text in *Goodnight Moon* provides a means of helping the child to separate from a parent at bedtime: "What could be more in keeping with helping the child to acquire—through simple language, plot, poetry and picture—the pleasure of separation from a parent, to the natural embrace of sleep, to the stars and to the quiet night. Learning to be alone in the company of a reading parent is dress rehearsal for the real thing." If we take time to look at Clement Hurd's illustrations with a critical eye, we can see how he managed to get this sense across in his artwork as he interpreted the surface elements in the story.

Hurd sets up a predictable pattern by alternating color full-page spreads illustrating the bedroom with pages on which details from the room (a bedside table, two kittens, etc.) are shown in shades of gray. This pattern adds variety and interest but it also serves to illuminate the theme of Brown's text, as the achromatic pages help the child viewer focus on pieces of the whole as separate entities.

The color pages illustrate essentially the same scene over and over again with subtle shifts in perspective. This lends a sense of visual harmony that slows down the pace of what would surely be a rapid-fire story if the perspective jumped around from place to place in the room. Straight horizontal lines dominate the composition, leading the viewer's eye to sweep across the page, taking in the enumerated objects in the room. These contrast with a more subtle, diagonal line emanating from a lighted lamp that points right at the restless child in bed. The eye is also drawn to the rounded shapes that dominate the center of each picture: a large oval-shaped rug and a hearth with a burning fire. These comforting cozy shapes fill the distance between the child and the mother, suggesting that although they are separated from each other, they are still connected.

A subtle gradation in value occurs throughout the book in the color spreads, as the room grows darker with every turn of the page. We see gradation in shape as the moon slowly moves across the night sky outside the bedroom window. Both show the natural passage of time.

Hurd also uses balance to create a sense of comfort and security. The strong horizontal line that cuts across the center of each double-page spread represents the line between the walls, which are green, and the floor, which is red. Since red and green are complementary colors, this gives the scene a formal balance. They also provide a balance between warm and cool colors, which might reflect the child's mixed emotions about bedtime.

The achromatic pages show balance as well. The initial pages balance each other by showing different objects of similar size and shape on opposing pages. To accomplish this, Hurd surrounds the objects with amorphous shapes, but as the story progresses, the shapes grow smaller and less like each other, moving from a symmetrical to an asymmetrical balance until we get to the delightfully surprising spread that places "nobody" (a blank page) opposite a bowl of mush. The next achromatic page restores perfect balance in a double-page spread that shows the comforting, familiar horizon of a clear night sky. We might ask ourselves, why did the artist do this? What effect does it have? Does it merely serve the purpose of illustrating details of the child's bedroom? Or was the artist aiming for something more? If we think about what happens to balance in the pictures and relate it to the action of the story—a child trying to delay sleep by saying goodnight to everything he sees in his room—we might speculate that Hurd uses the achromatic pictures to symbolize the process of falling asleep. In the beginning everything is clear and orderly, but things gradually get smaller and more dreamlike. We sink slowly into nothingness (the blank page) and have a momentary flash of wakefulness in which we see a bowl of mush on the bedside table. In the end, sleep takes over as an endless horizon of the world outside the bedroom window.

By looking closely at just one principle then—balance—we can see that Clement Hurd's illustrations for *Goodnight Moon* not only complement the story but actually clarify its meaning in a way that the simple words cannot. They are an integral part of the book and contribute greatly to its success over the decades. And, remarkably, they do it all without being flashy or calling attention to themselves.

MEDIA

An artist chooses a medium, such as paint, ink, or cut paper, to project a desired effect. Some artists feel more comfortable working with one medium and they use it in every book they illustrate. Others use different media for different books. In recent years a lot of attention has been placed on artistic media by reviewers, and many have demanded more information from the publishers. In response, some publishers place a note about the medium used to create the illustrations on the book's title page verso. Interesting as these notes may be, it is not really essential to be able to distinguish between gouache and tempera paint in evaluating or commenting about art. It is more important to notice how the use of paint affects the artistic expression as a whole. Still, in deference to the media watchers, I will define the various media most commonly used in children's book art, giving examples of books in which they are used.

Media can be broadly broken down into those that use *drawing,* those that use *painting,* those that use *print-making,* those that use *collage,* and those that use *photography.* Combinations of any two or more of these are referred to as *mixed media.* With the technological changes in printing over the past decade, there has been more reliance on painting and less on drawing and printmaking. Drawing and printmaking emphasize the drawn line and therefore create a *linear style,* whereas paint emphasizes color and tone, a style aptly referred to as *painterly.* Both collage and photography emphasize form and volume, which gives a three-dimensional quality to the art.

DRAWING

Drawing allows for a wide range of styles and expressions through the use of line and value. Lines can express emotion and movement. They can be light and humorous or heavy and serious. Value conveys depth and volume. The most common media used for drawing are:

Pen and ink: Makes strong, sure lines that create lively characters and clearly defined settings. Pen and ink is often used to draw pictures that are then colored with paint such as watercolor. James Stevenson is a master at using sketchy pen-and-ink lines to express character in books such as Helen V. Griffith's *Grandaddy's Place* (Greenwillow, 1987). William Steig also uses pen and ink with watercolor in *Doctor De Soto* (Farrar, 1982). His firm, expressive outlines emphasize the humorous interplay between characters.

Pencil or graphite: Allows for a full range of value from light to dark to create different moods and a sense of depth. Stephen Gammell used pencil to illustrate Olaf Baker's *Where the Buffaloes Begin* (Warne, 1981) and a combination of graphite and colored pencil to illustrate Cynthia Rylant's *The Relatives Came* (Bradbury, 1984).

Pastel: Powder color, mixed to the desired hue with white chalk and bound with tragacanth and liquids, is solidly packed and used in a form that resembles chalk. It has a soft, opaque quality, as is apparent in Chris Van Allsburg's pastel illustrations for his book *The Wreck of the Zephyr* (Houghton, 1983).

Scratchboard: Rather than drawing per se, the artist uses a sharp instrument to scratch an illustration into a two-layered black-and-white or black-and-multicolored board. Brian Pinkney works almost exclusively in scratchboard. In Robert D. San Souci's *The Faithful*

Friend (Simon & Schuster, 1995) he overpainted the illustrations with oil to add color to the sharp black-and-white contrasts.

PAINTING

Painting uses color above all other elements to convey meaning and emotions. Many types of paint are used in picture books. Each begins as a finely ground pigment that is mixed with a different type of binder to adhere to a surface, and as such has its own distinctive properties.

Gouache: Powder color mixed with an opaque white. Vivid colors express the sheer joy of living in Vera B. Williams' *More More More, Said the Baby: 3 Love Stories* (Greenwillow, 1990).

Poster paint: A coarser version of gouache because the color pigment is not as finely ground. The paintings in *Ten, Nine, Eight* (Greenwillow, 1983) by Molly Bang use contrasting colors to create a sense of excitement, while rounded shapes convey security.

Tempera: Powder color ground in water and mixed with an albuminous, gelatinous, or colloidal medium. Leo Lionni used broad strokes of tempera to create flat patterns that echoed the traditional art of India for his picture book *Tico and the Golden Wings* (Pantheon, 1964).

Watercolor: Powder color bound with gum arabic and glycerine. It is a transparent medium applied with water. By far the most popular medium among children's book artists who use paint, watercolor opens the door to a tremendous range of expression. Artists can use it to portray quiet, somber scenes or the activity on a crowded, busy street. Watercolor is an effective medium for detailed portrayals of people and animals. Jerry Pinkney used the whole range to his advantage in his intricately detailed paintings for Julius Lester's *John Henry* (Dial, 1994).

Oil paint: Powder color mixed with linseed oil. It can be applied thickly to a surface to create texture. Paul O. Zelinsky used oil paint in the Brothers Grimm's *Hansel and Gretel* (Dodd, Mead, 1984) to capture the feeling of seventeenth-century Dutch genre paintings.

Acrylic: Powder color mixed with water-based plastic. Like oil paint, it can be applied thickly to create a textured surface. Barbara Cooney's acrylic paintings in Donald Hall's *Ox-Cart Man* (Viking, 1979) maintain a consistent value throughout to give them the characteristic flat appearance of naive art.

PRINTMAKING

In printmaking, the artist creates a negative, backward image on a surface other than paper, such as wood, linoleum, cardboard, metal, or stone. The surface is then inked and pressed against paper so that the image is transferred to the paper. The very earliest children's books, illustrated with woodcut prints, date back to the sixteenth century, and we have many strong examples of the various printmaking techniques in twentieth-century picture books. With the advances in printing technology, however, printmaking may be classified as an endangered art form in picture books. One notable holdout is the artist Arthur

Geisert, who continues to create stunning picture books illustrated with etchings, such as *The Ark* (Houghton, 1988) and its sequel, *After the Flood* (Houghton, 1994).

COLLAGE

Fragments of paper, fabric, and other material are glued to a background paper to create collage. Because the fragments are often of made up of varying substances and thicknesses, collage accentuates texture. It also encourages viewers to look closely at the pieces as well as at the composition as a whole. For both of these reasons, collage was a brilliant choice as a medium for Ed Young's *Seven Blind Mice* (Philomel, 1992). In this East Indian fable about seven characters who each "see" a different part of an elephant by touching it, Young has cleverly used a different kind of paper for each mouse's personal vision.

PHOTOGRAPHY

Photography is frequently used as an illustration medium in nonfiction books for children. We see it used to illustrate children's picture books as well, especially concept books. Tana Hoban has raised the use of photography to an art form in her books about shape, color, size, and texture, which encourage children to look for order in the world around them. Bruce McMillan and Margaret Miller have followed Hoban's lead, and although their concept books are a bit more obvious, they are no less compelling to children who enjoy photographic images. Nina Crews combines photography and collage to create exciting images of a child at play in an urban neighborhood in *One Hot Summer Day* (Greenwillow, 1995).

STYLE

Style can refer to the features that make an individual artist's work distinctive and recognizable. It can also refer to a particular manner of artistic expression that has been developed over time and that can be defined by broad characteristics. In written reviews of picture books, the identification of a particular art style can be very helpful to readers who are trying to get a sense of what the art looks like. If we read that the illustrations are realistic, for example, it can help us begin to picture them.

Realistic: Illustrations that attempt to depict things the way they really look. Objects and people are shown in proper perspective and proportion. John Steptoe's *Mufaro's Beautiful Daughters* (Lothrop, 1987) is a good example of a realistic style.

Abstract: The artist deliberately distorts perspective and proportion so that objects and people are removed from reality. There are hundreds of examples of the use of abstraction in picture books. An especially outstanding example is *Yo! Yes?* (Orchard, 1993) by Chris Raschka, which heightens emotion and meaning through the use of abstracted human shapes, cleverly echoed with abstracted language.

Surrealistic: Realistic art that achieves a dreamlike quality or sense of unreality through unnatural or unexpected juxtapositions of objects or people. Anthony Browne's picture book *Changes* (Knopf, 1990) brilliantly uses a surreal style to show a young boy's difficult adjustment to his new baby sister.

Nonobjective: Part of the contemporary art movement, nonobjective art gets away from the idea of depicting objects and people at all and instead uses color, texture, line, and shape to suggest expression and mood. This style is used infrequently in children's picture books, although you will sometimes see it used in backgrounds. Ashley Bryan incorporates a nonobjective style into the backgrounds of many of his paintings in picture books. See, for example, *All Night, All Day* (Atheneum, 1991).

Impressionistic: A highly influential style developed by nineteenth-century French painters who used dabs of color to re-create a sense of reflected, or broken, light. Impressionists concerned themselves with the changing effect of light on surfaces to capture a subjective or sensory impression of a scene or object rather than a detailed depiction of reality. Maurice Sendak used this style in his artwork for Charlotte Zolotow's *Mr. Rabbit and the Lovely Present* (Harper, 1962).

Expressionistic: An influential twentieth-century movement developed into a style that expresses the artist's personal response to the subject. It is closely related to abstract art. Since it is concerned primarily with the emotions, it is widely used in picture books. Vera Williams'

A Chair for My Mother (Greenwillow, 1982) provides one of many examples.

Naive: Depicts scenes out of the artist's own experiences in what appears to be an untrained, awkward style. There is no depth in the pictures, and all people and objects appear flat and one-dimensional. Mattie Lou O'Kelley is a well-known naive artist whose paintings have been arranged into picture-book accounts of her life, such as *From the Hills of Georgia: An Autobiography in Paintings* (Little, Brown, 1983). Picture-book artist Barbara Cooney has used the naive art style in several books that cover the life spans of ordinary fictional characters. For an example see *Ox-Cart Man*.

Folk art: There are many variants in folk art style, as each is developed in a particular time and place and reflects the aesthetic values of the culture from which it comes. What they all have in common is a striking use of color, lack of perspective, the use of stylized pattern, and simple shapes. Folk art in its pure form has been used in picture books such as Percy Trezise and Dick Roughsey's *Gidja the Moon* (Gareth Stevens, 1988), which employs a symbolic style native to Australia, and Arthur Dorros' *Tonight Is Carnaval* (Dutton, 1991), which is illustrated with *arpilleras*, traditional wall hangings stitched by indigenous women in Lima, Peru. Other artists have used styles inspired by folk art. For example, Nancy Hom based her paintings for Blia Xiong's folktale *Nine in One Grr! Grr!: A Folktale from the Hmong People of Laos* (Children's Book Press, 1989), on the style used by the Hmong people in their embroidered story cloths. The style Paul Goble uses in all his retellings of Lakota folk-tales was inspired by traditional nineteenth-century Lakota ledger art, an art tradition started by imprisoned Lakota warriors who drew detailed accounts of battles in ledger books.

Cartoon art: The artist uses line to create stock characters marked by exaggeration and absurdity. This style is widely used in humorous picture books that contain a lot of slapstick action. Steven Kellogg uses a cartoon style almost exclusively in his picture books, such as the ever-popular *The Day Jimmy's Boa Ate the Wash* by Trinka Hakes Noble (Dial, 1980). Many artists combine it with design elements popularized in comic strips, by using sequences of panels and speech balloons in their compositions. James Stevenson uses these techniques in a number of his books. For an example, see *There's Nothing to Do* (Greenwillow, 1986) or any other of his picture books featuring the delightfully daring character Grandpa. Cartoon art is also frequently used to lighten a heavy subject and to put a comfortable distance between the child reader and a potentially disturbing theme. Steven Björkman uses a cartoon style effectively for this purpose in his illustrations for Ellen Levine's *I Hate English!* (Scholastic, 1989), the story of an immigrant child's difficult adjustment to life in the United States.

For every picture book an artist chooses the medium and style she thinks will best serve the story. Many artists vary both medium and style from book to book: John Steptoe and Ed Young come immediately to mind as two artists whose picture books reflect an enormous versatility in both areas. Other artists choose to use the same medium and style again and again, and offer us a visual showcase of variations on a theme. Whatever the case, think about how the chosen medium and style works in a picture book you are evaluating. How is the medium used to express the action or emotion in the story? Is it effective? Does the art style match the textual style? If not, is there a reason for this incongruity? Picture-book creators sometimes purposely contrast the visual and verbal tone in a story for the sake of irony. A direct, understated text may be illustrated with scenes filled with action and wild antics, so that the story springs from the deliberate conflict between the two. Peggy Rathmann did this brilliantly in *Officer Buckle and Gloria* (Putnam, 1995).

In spite of the great feeling of surprise and spontaneity we often get from them, it is important to remember that nothing ever happens accidentally in a picture book. It is a complex, carefully planned work of art that creates a satisfying interplay between text and pictures to tell a story that a small child can understand. By learning to look for the individual pieces and by developing an awareness of the techniques that are used to make them all work together, we can better understand the work as a whole, so that we can clearly articulate our critical and emotional responses.

CHAPTER 6

Easy Readers and Transitional Books

It is a common misconception among many adults that picture books are the best books to give a child who is just learning to read. While it is true that some picture books have characteristics that make them accessible to beginning readers, most picture books, since they are intended to be read aloud to children, are written at a reading level much higher than that of a child in first grade. There are, however, books that are expressly written for children who are learning to read, which use simple vocabulary, large typeface, and short sentences. These are called *easy readers, beginning readers,* or simply *readers.* One step up from readers is another category of books that are most commonly called *transitional books.* These books feature simple sentences and short chapters, and serve as a bridge between easy readers and longer chapter books.

Both beginning readers and transitional books are

relatively new to the scene in children's trade publishing. In 1954 novelist John Hersey wrote an article in *Life* magazine in which he complained that children in public schools were failing to learn to read because their schoolbooks were bland and unchallenging. He described the characters in these primers as "abnormally courteous and unnaturally clean boys and girls" and the illustrations as uniform and insipid. "Why should [children] not have pictures that widen rather than narrow the associative richness the children give to the words they illustrate—drawings like those wonderfully imaginative geniuses among children's illustrators—Tenniel, Howard Pyle, Dr. Seuss . . . ?"

Soon after the article appeared in print, Dr. Seuss took up the challenge put forth by Hersey. He acquired a limited-vocabulary list from the textbook division at Houghton Mifflin and spent more than a year shaping just 237 easy-to-read words into a story. The result was the now-classic *Cat in the Hat*, published by Random House in 1957. Although Hersey had been thinking of illustrations in particular when he cited Dr. Seuss, in the end it was the book's text that stood out as remarkable. Dr. Seuss showed that with a little creativity and a lot of hard work, engaging stories could be written with a controlled vocabulary.

That same year Harper & Row came out with *Little Bear* by Else Holmelund Minarik, the first title in its influential "I Can Read" series. While Seuss set the standard for excellence in writing, the "I Can Read" series set the standard for form. Recognizing that children learning to read are anxious to feel like "big kids," Harper designed the books in their beginning reader series to look like skinny chapter books rather than picture books. *Little Bear*, in fact, is divided into four chapters that serve not only to give young readers natural stopping places for much-needed breaks from the hard work of reading, but also help to build the self-esteem of children who pride themselves in reading chapters. The characteristic design of the "I Can Read" series was imitated by many other publishers as they launched their own beginning reader series in subsequent years, and today it is widely recognized as a standard form.

In the 1970s Arnold Lobel took beginning readers to new heights with the introduction of his "Frog and Toad" series. Separate volumes in this series have been cited as Honor Books by both the Newbery and the Caldecott Committees, an indication of the overall excellence of the "Frog and Toad" books, since beginning readers are rarely singled out as distinguished for either writing or art. Using a limited vocabulary, Lobel managed to create two distinctive characters by zeroing in on their simple interactions with each other. Their actions and reactions are often based on repetition, a device that not only makes the text predictable and easy to read but also allows the author to introduce surprising, humorous elements to balance the predictability. In *Frog and Toad Are Friends* (Harper, 1970), for example, Frog asks Toad to tell him a story to cheer him up when he is sick. Toad seeks inspiration in unusual ways:

> *Then Toad went into the house*
> *and stood on his head.*

"Why are you standing
on your head?" asked Frog.
"I hope that if I stand on my head,
it will help me
to think of a story," said Toad.

Toad stood on his head
for a long time.
But he could not think
of a story to tell Frog.

Then Toad poured a glass of water
over his head.
"Why are you pouring water
over your head?" asked Frog.
"I hope that if I pour water
over my head,
it will help me to think
of a story," said Toad.
Toad poured many glasses of water
over his head.
But he could not think
of a story to tell Frog.

Then Toad began
to bang his head
against the wall.
"Why are you banging your head
against the wall?" asked Frog.
"I hope that if I bang my head

against the wall hard enough,
it will help me to think of a story,"
said Toad.

Each of Toad's unpredictable actions is clearly shown in the illustrations. These pictures give clues to the reader who is struggling to decode the words. Throughout the "Frog and Toad" books, Lobel provides a comfortable context for beginning readers with both words and pictures. His words provide clues by using repetition, and his pictures provide clues by depicting action. As beginning readers, these books represent the perfect unity of form and content.

Unfortunately there has not been a similar progression in the development of books written for children at the next stage in their reading. Parents, teachers, and librarians had for a long time been stressing a need for what they called "third-grade books"—books that offered a little more challenge than the hardest easy readers and yet were still a bit easier than the easiest chapter books. Children who were making the transition from easy readers to chapter books were beginning to read mainly for meaning, and yet reading was still hard work for their untrained eyes. They needed books that struck a delicate balance between readers and chapter books. Although most publishers' lists offered at least a few titles that fit into this category, there was no consistent effort to specifically create this type of book until the mid-1980s.

An outstanding forerunner of transitional books, and one that many hoped would set the standard, was Ann Cameron's *The Stories Julian Tells* (Pantheon, 1981). This easy chapter book featuring an imaginative young African-American boy and his trusting, gullible little brother, Huey, was perfectly designed for children making the transition from easy readers to chapter books. Like many easy readers, it has a large typeface, and the number of lines per page never exceeds fifteen. But *The Stories Julian Tells* is designed to look like a thick chapter book, the sort of book that readers making the transition are desperate to be able to read. Many librarians who have had the opportunity to introduce these young readers to Julian have seen this scene played out again and again: As the librarian pulls the book off the shelf, the child hesitates upon seeing its thickness. The moment the book is opened, however, the child shows visible relief, then delight, then pride. Because adults saw this happen repeatedly with a variety of young readers, soon after *The Stories Julian Tells* was published, they asked for several dozen more like it.

A few years later, when publishers began to develop series to meet these demands, *The Stories Julian Tells* and its follow-up, *More Stories Julian Tells* (Knopf, 1986), were not used as models, unfortunately. Publishers opted instead for a standard design that made the books look like skinny chapter books. In order to accomplish this, more text had to be crammed onto each page by using smaller type and more lines per page. Even subsequent volumes in Cameron's "Julian" series adopted this new look, rather than following the standard for excellence set by the first two books in the series.

The success of both easy readers and transitional books is as much dependent on form as it is on content. Because these books are created especially to meet the needs of children who are developing reading skills, it is helpful for us to have a minimal basic understanding of what happens when a child begins to read, so that we can apply this knowledge to the books when we evaluate them. Most children learn to read in the controlled setting of a classroom, and they are often taught using basal readers that are specially designed for this purpose. Easy readers and transitional books were not specifically created to replace the basal reader; rather, they were intended as supplementary reading so that children can practice newly acquired skills and find a wide range of reading material that interests them.

Children who are beginning to read are learning to decode printed symbols that stand for words within their oral vocabulary. To decode the words, they sound them out or say them aloud so that they can hear them. As children learn to read, they develop a store of *sight words*, common words that they learn to recognize immediately, such as "the," "ball," "mother," "play," and "run." Sight words are most often consciously taught in the classroom; thus we get the concept of "reading at grade level."

Part of the challenge children face is in training their eyes to move from left to right across lines of print. The eye is controlled by small muscle movements, and for children small muscle movements are a challenge in and of themselves. When the eyes move across a line of print, they make a series of jumps, stopping briefly to focus. An experienced adult reader typically sees two letters to the left side of the point of focus and six to eight letters to the right. The inexperienced child reader, however, sees one letter to the left and one letter to the right of the point of focus. This physical reality explains why beginning readers find it easier to decode words made up of fewer than five letters. As their eye muscles begin to develop, they are gradually able to take in more on the right side of the point of focus and they can handle longer unfamiliar words. They can also begin to handle longer sentences. All the while they continue to add to their store of sight words. All these factors work together, so that with practice children eventually can make a shift from reading aloud to decode the words to reading silently for meaning.

The creators of easy readers and transitional books have taken this process into account in developing their books. They strive to meet the needs of children who are learning to read by paying special attention to both content and design. As we evaluate these books, we should look carefully at the following components of each:

Content: How is the story written to make it easy to read? What sort of vocabulary did the author choose to use? How often are difficult words used, and how does the author use them? How long are the sentences? Are the sentences simple, compound, or complex? How does the author use structure to build context and provide textual clues? How do the illustrations support the text and offer help to the reader?

Design: How is the text presented to make it easy to read? Is the type large and clear? Is there a lot of white space on the page? How long are the lines of type, and how many lines appear on the page? How often do illustrations appear, and how much space do they cover?

EASY READERS

When we evaluate easy readers, it is important to think about them in terms of what the author and illustrator have created (content) and how the publisher has presented the work of the author and illustrator (design). Both aspects should be given equal importance by the critic. In the best examples of this type of book, content and design form a unified whole that makes the task of reading easier and thus pleasurable for the child.

CONTENT
VOCABULARY

Most easy readers are written using the sight words children learn in first and second grade, combined with short words that are easy to decode. Compound words composed of two short sight words, such as "snowball," are also easier to read. Longer unfamiliar words can be successfully integrated in moderation if there are strong context clues in the pictures or if they are used as descriptors that can be skipped without losing meaning. In looking at the words appearing in easy readers, think about the kinds of words that are used. Are they sight words? If not, are they less than five letters? If they are long words, how are they used? Are there picture clues to help the child figure them out? Are the words likely to be part of the child's natural oral language? A word of three or four letters, such as "rue" or "cusp," isn't likely to mean anything to a six-year-old, even if it can be decoded. Notice the way Dr. Seuss ingeniously uses short words and sight vocabulary in this passage from *The Cat in the Hat*:

> *"Now look what you did!"*
> *Said the fish to the cat.*
> *"Now look at this house!*
> *Look at this! Look at that!*
> *You sank our toy ship,*
> *Sank it deep in the cake.*
> *You shook up our house*
> *And you bent our new rake."*

SENTENCE LENGTH

Children who are concentrating more on decoding the words than on the words' meaning need short declarative sentences, so that they haven't forgotten the beginning of the sentence by the time they reach the end of it. Sentences made up of five words are ideal for children just beginning to read, but those who are gaining skill and confidence can handle up to ten words per sentence. Even for more competent young readers, however, look for sentences of alternating lengths. An author may, for example, follow a long sentence with a succession of short sentences, as Edward Marshall does in the following passage from *Three by the Sea* (Dial, 1981).

> *One day a monster*
> *came out of the sea.*
> *He had big yellow eyes.*
> *He had sharp green teeth.*
> *He had long black claws.*
> *And he was really mean.*

Occasionally longer sentences can be used successfully if they can be broken up naturally into lines of shorter length, as in this sentence from *Little Bear:*

> *So Little Bear begins to make soup*
> *in the big black pot.*

Longer sentences can also work when a writer builds textual context using repetition, as Arnold Lobel does in the passage quoted earlier from *Frog and Toad Are Friends*, or when a writer uses rhyme, as Dr. Seuss did in *The Cat in the Hat.* Both of these devices serve to make the text more predictable and therefore easier to read.

In easy readers sentence length and structure are just as important as the vocabulary used to tell the story. When you evaluate this type of book, look at the sentences. How many words appear in them? If long sentences are used, are they alternated with short ones? Do you notice a lot of commas in the text? If so, this is often an indication of dependent clauses or extra information that makes the text harder to read. "Sam, a mean dog, bit my sister." is much more difficult to read than "Sam was a mean dog. He bit my sister."

PLOT

Beyond the constraints of language, easy readers fall into a broad range of categories, including nonfiction, folklore, poetry, science fiction, mysteries, historical fiction, animal fantasies, and realistic fiction, although the latter two make up the vast majority of what has been published to date.

The first page or two of an easy reader is especially important, because it must establish the context and stir children's interest enough to draw them into the story. Peggy Parish introduces the subject of dinosaurs in an easy reader this way:

> *Long, long ago*
> *the world was different.*
> *More land was under water.*
> *It was warm all the time.*
> *And dinosaurs*
> *were everywhere. . . .*

Notice how quickly Parish sets the scene with just a few sentences to introduce the topic and inspire young readers to turn the page to find out what happens next. Although she will go on to introduce more difficult words like "insects" and "enemies," she has wisely written the first two pages so that they will be very easy. This gives young readers the confidence they need to keep reading. Look closely at the first two or three pages of an easy reader as you evaluate it. Does it begin by using short sentences and simple concepts? Does it establish the setting and introduce the subject or characters quickly? Is it likely to make children want to turn the pages and keep reading?

Most stories in easy readers involve two or three main characters and have fast-moving plots with clear, direct action. Descriptive passages and internal motives are kept to a minimum. Many follow the pattern established by the "I Can Read" series and break the story up into four to six chapters. When this is done, chapters should be episodic; in other words, the action started at the beginning of a chapter is completed and brought to some sort of resolution at the end of the chapter. Each chapter, then, functions as a short story, and taken as a whole, all the chapters that make up one book have characters and setting in common.

Each of the four chapters in Minarik's *Little Bear* deals with the playful interactions between a mother bear and her small son. In chapter 1, Little Bear wants to go out to play in the snow, but he keeps returning to tell his mother he is cold and needs something warm to put on. She gives him a hat, a coat, and a pair of snow pants before suggesting he remove them all and wear his own nice warm fur coat outside. In chapter 2, Little Bear prepares a special birthday soup for himself as a succession of guests arrives for his party. Each one asks him what he is cooking, giving him an opportunity to describe repeatedly the wonders of birthday soup before Mother Bear comes home with a surprise birthday cake. In both of these chapters, episodes are built on a predictable accumulation of repeated actions that pave the way for a satisfying surprise ending. The character of an inventive and slightly dependent Little Bear is firmly established through his easy interactions with his patient, loving mother. After the first two chapters, young readers will feel familiar enough with the characters of Little Bear and his mother to easily follow the two final chapters, which break away from the predictable pattern of repetition. Like the first two chapters, however, chapters 3 and 4 center on Little Bear's actions, which elicit calm and satisfying reactions from his mother.

To evaluate the story line in an easy reader, look at each spread in it and notice what happens. There should be some action on every page. Are action verbs used to move the plot along? Are characters developed through interaction? Does the author use repeated actions in a creative way? Are surprises balanced with predictable elements?

ILLUSTRATIONS

Pictures in easy readers appear on every spread, and they generally vary in size from page to page. In addition to illustrating the story, they can give essential clues to help out with words or concepts that young readers may find difficult. When Cynthia Rylant tells us in *Henry and Mudge:*

The First Book (Bradbury, 1987) that the puppy Mudge grew out of seven collars in a row, artist Suçie Stevenson illustrates the seven collars and shows them in succession. This single illustration gives clues about the word "collar" and the concepts "grew out of" and "in a row." It also suggests just how big the tiny puppy grew to be, so that readers are prepared for a surprise when they see and read about the huge dog Mudge on the following page.

DESIGN

Because easy readers must meet meet the physical as well as intellectual needs of children who are learning to read, it is especially important to pay attention to design factors such as size of typeface, line length, space between words, space between lines, number of lines per page, amount of white space per page, and placement of illustrations.

SIZE OF TYPEFACE

Typography has its own system of measurement, based on *points*. A point is a little less than 1/72 of an inch. Most books for adults are set in typefaces of 10 to 12 points (the height of a capital letter). The standard size typeface for beginning readers is 18 points.

10 points

12 points

18 points

LINE LENGTH

By line length we mean the number of words per line. This line may be a complete sentence or it may be a phrase. Beginning readers should have lines between two and ten words in length. The longer the line, the more difficult it is for children to read. When you look at lines, you should also pay attention to where new sentences begin. New sentences beginning at the end of a line are harder for children to read.

SPACE BETWEEN WORDS

For inexperienced readers the space between words is just as important as the period at the end of the sentence is for experienced readers. They "read" the space as an indication of where one word ends and the next word begins. Spaces between words should be wide and clear.

SPACE BETWEEN LINES

There should be plenty of space between lines (*leading,* so called because old typesetting technology used strips of lead) in beginning readers, so that a child can easily keep his or her place in a line without wandering down into the next line. The more space between lines, the easier the text is to read. Most often leading is equal to the type size—that is, if the type is 18 point, there are 18 points of space between lines.

NUMBER OF LINES PER PAGE

Due to illustrations, this will vary from page to page, but in easy readers the number of lines per page should not exceed fifteen.

AMOUNT OF WHITE SPACE PER PAGE

Children work hard to decode the text in easy readers, and they need to rest their eyes frequently. A lot of white space around words and pictures gives their eyes a place to rest.

PLACEMENT OF ILLUSTRATIONS

In easy readers illustrations appear on every double-page spread. They may give essential picture clues to help the child, and they may provide little breaks for the eyes. They should not, however, overwhelm the reader by covering up every bit of white space, nor should they confuse the reader by taking over the text's territory. They are there to complement the text, not compete with it.

LEVELS

Easy readers fall roughly into three levels based on how easy or difficult they are for children to read. In evaluating an easy reader, it is very important for the critic to determine the level of the book by looking at elements of design and content. Although there are no hard-and-fast rules, and even formal readability scales such as Frye and Spache are not always reliable, we can make a general overall assessment of a book by taking concrete factors such as word usage, line length, sentence structure, and illustrations into consideration.

LEVEL ONE

The very easiest of the easy readers are written at a first-grade level. The text is set in 17- to 20-point type, and there are, on average, five words per line. The sentences average five to seven words, and the words that are used are largely sight vocabulary or one-syllable words of five letters or less. There are generally two to seven lines per page, with as much as two-thirds of each page used for illustrations and white space. The illustrations provide plenty of picture clues.

In P. D. Eastman's *Are You My Mother?* (Random House, 1960), for example, as a newly hatched baby bird searches for his mother, he comes across a kitten, a hen, a dog, a cow, a car, a boat, and a plane and asks each one in turn, "Are you my mother?" As each new animal or vehicle is introduced, it is shown clearly in the illustrations to provide a clue to the reader. Each one is also shown later on when the baby bird repeats his refrain: "The kitten was not his mother. The hen was not his mother," and so on as each new contender is added to the list. Eastman also uses plenty of repetition, not just of words and sentences but of actions, so that readers soon catch on that the baby bird will question every creature he encounters until he finally finds his rightful mother.

> *"Yes, I know who you*
> *are," said the baby bird.*
> *"You are not a kitten.*
> *"You are not a hen.*
> *"You are not a dog.*
> *"You are not a cow.*
> *"You are not a boat,*
> *or a plane, or a Snort!*
> *"You are a bird, and*
> *you are my mother."*

LEVEL TWO

Written at a second-grade level, easy readers in the middle range begin to use slightly more complex sentences, alternating them with short simple ones. The number of sight words has greatly expanded, and children can now handle occasional unfamiliar multisyllabic words that are part of their natural oral speech. No more than five words per line continues to be the ideal length, even though the sentences themselves can be longer. The number of lines per page varies from four to fifteen, and the text is fairly evenly balanced with illustrations or white space.

One of the perennial favorites for children at this level is Molly Garrett Bang's lively retelling of an African-American folktale, *Wiley and the Hairy Man: Adapted from an American Folk Tale* (Macmillan, 1976). In this

story a young boy outwits a monster three times by following instructions given him by his mother. Here is how
Bang describes their first meeting:

> *When Wiley looked up,*
> *there was the Hairy Man.*
> *He was coming through the*
> *trees. He sure was ugly.*
> *He was hairy all over.*
> *His eyes burned like coals.*
> *His teeth were big*
> *and sharp and white.*
> *He was swinging a sack.*
>
> *Wiley was scared.*
> *Quick as he could,*
> *he climbed up a*
> *big bay tree.*

Bang cleverly uses the device of repetition in each of
Wiley's three encounters with the Hairy Man: She
includes dialogue in which Wiley's mother tells him what
to do if he should meet the Hairy Man and follows it with
a passage that describes their actual meeting and shows
Wiley acting on his mother's wise instructions.

LEVEL THREE

The most challenging of the easy readers are written at
a level that is typical of children who are beginning third

grade. Due to the use of more difficult words, an adult reading the text may not even be aware that the book is written with controlled vocabulary. There is a greater frequency of compound and complex sentences, resulting in language that begins to sound more natural. Still, the line lengths are short, less than eight words, and the number of lines per page does not exceed fifteen. The text may cover up to three quarters of the page, although due to the large type and plenty of space between lines, there is a lot of white space on each page. Illustrations may even appear only on alternating pages, and they begin to function more as decorations.

Note the characteristics of a Level Three reader in this passage from *Witch, Goblin and Ghost Are Back* (Pantheon, 1985) by Sue Alexander:

> *He dangled his feet in the water*
> *and wiggled his toes.*
> *"Hmmmm," he said.*
> *"If I am gone for a long time,*
> *Ghost may forget*
> *that I like to hear his stories.*
> *And Witch may forget*
> *that I like to eat her fudge."*
> *Goblin pulled his feet*
> *out of the water.*
>
> *"Oh no!" he shouted.*
> *"If I am gone for a very long time,*
> *Witch and Ghost may forget ME!"*

Goblin jumped up.
He took hold of the steering pole
and steered the raft back
the other way.

Children who are comfortably reading Level Three texts are probably ready to make the jump to the next highest level: the transitional book. This transitional stage in a child's reading life is usually brief, but it is very important. It is during this stage that the child gains confidence and discovers that reading is personally important and pleasurable.

TRANSITIONAL BOOKS

As noted earlier, there has not been the careful attention given to the design of transitional books as there has to easy readers. *The Stories Julian Tells* sets a standard for excellence in design that few have matched (or even striven for). Like easy readers, it has a large typeface and the number of lines per page never exceeds fifteen. The number of words per line, however, has been increased to an average of eight to twelve. Sentences are no longer broken down into shorter lines, and right margins are justified. There is plenty of white space on every page, with generous margins at the top, bottom, and sides, and there is still a full line of leading after every line of type. The book includes frequent full-page black-and-white illustrations, but there may be two or three spreads in a row with no illustrations at all. The six chapters are short and episodic, varying in length from seven to seventeen pages. It is the length of the chapters, the justified right margins, and the smaller ratio of text to illustrations that give *The Stories Julian Tells* the look of a chapter book, while design elements such as line length, type size, and white space make it accessible to inexperienced readers.

Compare the first to the third book in the "Julian" sequence, *Julian's Glorious Summer* (Random House, 1987). The latter was designed to conform to the publisher's then-new transitional series, "Stepping Stone." The third "Julian" book uses a much smaller typeface and has up to twenty-five lines per page. This design is much more typical of what we see in publishers' series of transitional books.

There are several other characteristics these books have in common that make them more accessible to newly independent readers:

1) A simple vocabulary without too many surprising descriptors or multisyllabic words. Children at this stage of reading are beginning to read for meaning, so it is important that the words they are reading mean something to them. What words has the author used? Are they common, everyday words a seven- or eight-year-old is likely to know? If the meaning of a word is likely to be unfamiliar, has the author provided a context that will give clues to the reader?

Ann Cameron included a chapter about a fig tree in *The Stories Julian Tells*. While transitional readers would not have any trouble reading the word *fig,* Cameron must have been aware that there would be some children who had never seen or eaten a fresh fig. Notice how skillfully she provides a context for those children so that they will not be excluded:

> *In the summer I like to lie in the grass and look at clouds and eat figs. Figs are soft and purple and delicious. Their juice runs all over my face, and I eat them till I'm so full I can't eat any more.*

2) Sentences that are relatively short, direct, and uncomplicated. Pay close attention to sentence length. Do long sentences alternate with short ones? How are longer sentences constructed? Compound sentences are easier to read, and complex sentences with dependent clauses are more difficult. Do you see more than a few commas per page? If so, that may be an indication that more complicated sentences are being used, as commas often set off dependent clauses.

Compare the following passages. The first is from Ellen Conford's *A Job for Jenny Archer* (Little, Brown, 1989) and the second from S. E. Hinton's *The Puppy Sister* (Delacorte, 1995):

> *The big black dog shot out the door. Wilson gulped. Barkley flew down the steps and ran right at him.*
> *He forgot he wasn't afraid of Barkley anymore. He forgot that*

Barkley loved him. He forgot that
all Barkley wanted to do was lick
his face. [Conford]

Even though I could see out, there
wasn't much to see. Just the back of
the front seat, but I didn't care
because there were too many sounds—
cars and trucks rushing by, honking,
the engine of our car. And too many
smells—gasoline, Nick, Nick's Chee-
tos, Mom and Dad, and then bursts
of smells as we passed farms and
ranches and towns. [Hinton]

Even though the passage from *The Puppy Sister* uses simple vocabulary, the sentence structure is quite complex and would require the skills of a more experienced reader. Because this sort of complexity is common in the book, we would not classify it as a book for transitional readers, even though it has many of the characteristics we look for: large, clear typeface; plenty of white space; occasional illustrations; and short, episodic chapters.

3) Brief episodes, chapters, or intervals that stand out to the reader. The average length of a chapter in a transitional book is just six to eight pages. Each chapter typically follows the actions of one, two, or three characters in one place at one time. Each of the chapters in Betsy Byars' *Beans on the Roof* (Delacorte, 1988), for example, centers on a different member of the Bean family going up to the roof to write a poem. The setting changes in each chapter of *Pinky and Rex and the Bully* (Atheneum, 1996) by James Howe, but each chapter is limited to one main action that moves the plot along.

Chapter 1: Pinky's first encounter with the bully

Chapter 2: Pinky discusses the problem with his neighbor, Mrs. Morgan

Chapter 3: Pinky's second encounter with the bully

Chapter 4: Pinky discusses the problem with his father

Chapter 5: Pinky decides on a course of action and discusses it with Mrs. Morgan

Chapter 6: Pinky's third and final encounter with the bully

Chapter 7: Pinky shares his success with Mrs. Morgan

Look at each chapter to see exactly what happens. Can it be easily summed up in a few words? If not, it will probably be too difficult for transitional readers.

Inexperienced readers often have a great deal of trouble grasping jumps in time and changes in setting. These are two very important elements in fiction writing, and children need to gain familiarity with them in order to become competent readers of fiction. Because chapters are short in transitional books, changes in time and setting generally occur between rather than within chapters. These changes will not be obvious to young readers unless they are given clear, direct descriptions. Phrases such as "The next day . . ." and "When Sam got to the park . . ." are essential.

In *The Chalk Box Kid* (Random House, 1987) Clyde

Robert Bulla always lets his readers know exactly where and when the action takes place by building it into the opening paragraph of the chapter. For example:

> Chapter 1: *Gregory heard the clock strike. It was an hour till midnight. His birthday would soon be over.*

> Chapter 5: *Gregory's second week in the new school began with a party. It was for Ivy.*

> Chapter 9: *But it was hard for him to go to school the next day. When he got there, he walked around the block before he went in.*

Look for changes in time and setting. Where and how often do they occur? Does the author use helpful descriptive phrases to let readers know exactly where and when the action takes place?

4) Content compelling enough to hold a child's interest but not so complicated that it's hard to follow. Like easy readers, transitional books generally have two or three main characters and brisk plots with a lot of action. Contemporary stories about friends and family work especially well, because the types of characters, situations, and conflicts they offer are familiar and easily understood by newly independent readers. More whimsical elements can be introduced if they are firmly rooted in a reality that children will easily absorb. Irina Korschunow, for example, offers children an engaging psychological fantasy in *Adam Draws Himself a Dragon* (Harper, 1986) that succeeds as a transitional book largely because the dragon Adam creates is fascinated by very ordinary human activities: singing, drawing, writing, reading, eating chocolate, going to school, turning somersaults, and climbing trees. Each chapter involves the dragon demanding that Adam teach him one of these human skills, and by doing so, Adam gradually gains self-confidence himself.

Like Adam, children who are going through this stage in their lives as readers need to build self-confidence as they make the leap from easy readers to chapter books. Transitional books serve as a bridge for them. It is a bridge that some children will cross very quickly; others will have to linger for a while. The best transitional books will suggest that the trip across is worth it and that great things await them on the other side.

Fiction

hildren's fiction offers a rich diversity of style, content, and form to satisfy a variety of tastes, interests, and abilities of young readers. From the witty portrayals of ordinary child life in Beverly Cleary's "Ramona" books to Gary Paulsen's gripping stories of wilderness survival to the complexities of character revealed in Virginia Hamilton's multilayered novels, there are books to amuse, stimulate, and captivate many types of readers.

With such a wide range of fiction, how do we choose the best? What characterizes an outstanding novel for children? Are there literary standards that we can apply to all works of fiction? How can we tell what will appeal to children at different age levels and abilities? Can a fourth grader read the same books as a seventh grader? Do boys and girls like the same kinds of books? How important is popularity and child appeal? Why don't they give the Newbery Medal to R. L. Stine? What's the problem with series books, anyway? If kids are reading them, isn't that the most important thing?

These are all questions commonly asked by people who are thinking about children's fiction. All are valid and important questions for us to consider. Many of them have their roots in the conflicting points of view that led to the creation of contemporary children's fiction in the first place.

Prior to the 1920s, most of children's fiction consisted of popular series books, such as "Tom Swift," "The Motor Girls," "The Bobbsey Twins," and dozens of other series written according to a prescribed formula. There were no separate children's divisions in publishing houses at the time, and even children's departments in public libraries were a rarity.

In the early part of the twentieth century libraries began to establish specialized departments for children by hiring women who had been trained in a newly developing field devoted to children's services. But when these librarians looked for books to add to their libraries' collections, they found that there was little that met their critical standards. In 1920 Anne Carroll Moore, the influential head of the New York Public Library's Children's Department, lamented: "We are tired of substitutes for realities in writing for children. The trail . . . [is] strewn with patronage and propaganda, moralizing self-sufficiency and sham efficiency, mock heroics and cheap optimism — above all, with the commonplace in theme, treatment, and language."

Of course, there were books such as *The Adventures of*

Tom Sawyer, Little Women, and *Hans Brinker, Or, the Silver Skates,* but these titles were the exception, not the rule. Thanks to the combined efforts of children's librarians, publishers, and booksellers, the rules were about to change.

In the United States just after the end of World War I, great changes were in the air. Within a five-year period (1919–1924) there was a remarkable series of events that would have a long-lasting impact: Children's divisions were set up in publishing houses; *The Horn Book* magazine was founded; Children's Book Week was established; and, perhaps most importantly, the John Newbery Medal was created to encourage writers and publishers to produce high-quality books for children.

Of course, this radical change in children's books was not without its detractors. The proponents and producers of formula series books launched a verbal attack on children's librarians, claiming that since they were mere women (and spinsters at that), they had no right to judge what was fit reading for red-blooded American boys. Librarians, in alliance with the Boy Scouts of America, countered by emphasizing "good books for boys" in their early recommendations, thus advancing the notion of gender-specific reading tastes.

The first several winners of the Newbery Medal are a case in point. They are for the most part titles that would be touted as books for boys. Speaking about the work of 1924 Newbery Medalist Charles Boardman Hawes, shortly after the announcement had been made, librarian Louise P. Latimer stated: "Let us nail them to our mast and say to those who question or discredit our judgment, these are examples of good writing for boys. Match them with hack writing if you can."

Children's librarians quickly established themselves as the major influence in setting the literary standards for children's fiction. Formula series fiction faded into the background, and although it has never completely died out, it has been greatly marginalized.

Over the past several decades a significant body of outstanding fiction written especially for children has developed. It can be categorized by genre as realism, fantasy, science fiction, or mystery, but all children's novels have certain elements in common. When we evaluate children's fiction, we can look closely at plot, characterization, point of view, setting, style, and theme.

PLOT

The basis of all fiction is the *plot*—that is, a series of events that tell the story, actions that are linked by cause and effect, so that the pieces of the story are all tied together by a narrative. Unlike real life, everything that happens in a story has a recognizable purpose. If, for example, a notebook is left on the school bus in chapter 1, we know that something is going to happen as a result; otherwise, the author wouldn't have mentioned it.

NARRATIVE STRUCTURE

Narrative order refers to the order in which the events take place. Most children's novels follow a direct linear pattern, with events occurring in **chronological order**. They may take place over a period of just a few days, a month, or years. *The Midwife's Apprentice* (Clarion, 1995) by Karen Cushman provides a good example of a straight-forward narrative as it traces the development of a homeless waif from one spring to the next after she is taken in by the town midwife. Throughout the novel the author makes frequent references to the seasonal passage of time, not only to make the progression of time clear to young readers but also to symbolize Beetle's growth.

A slightly more complex form of narrative order based on chronology is one that tells the story from the point of view of more than one character. Kevin Henkes uses this device effectively in *Words of Stone* (Greenwillow, 1992) by telling portions of the story from the point of view of a ten-year-old boy named Blaze and the rest from that of Joselle, a girl his age who is spending the summer at her grandmother's house, next door to Blaze. Since it is a little more difficult for children to follow this kind of order, authors can make it easier, as Henkes did, by shifting the viewpoint between, rather than within, chapters and by using the characters' names as chapter headings so that young readers know from the outset which character is speaking.

More complex still is the use of **flashbacks**, in which the author disrupts a linear chronology to recount events that occurred at an earlier time, usually to give readers insight into character. This sort of narrative order can be very difficult for less experienced child readers to follow, as they expect events to happen in a chronological sequence and will struggle to fit the past events into the present. For them the flashback needs to be clearly framed in some way, so that they understand the shift in time. Sharon Creech accomplished this in *Walk Two Moons* (Harper, 1994) by introducing the flashbacks as a series of brief episodes in a continuing story that thirteen-year-old Salamanca tells her grandparents on a cross-country car trip. With frequent interruptions from Sal's grandparents, young readers never lose sight of where they are in time; in a sense, the flashbacks seem to occur in the present, since they are part of a story being told in the present.

CONFLICT

Conflict is a major element of plot that keeps the story moving and stirs the interest of the reader, who wants to find out what happens next and how the conflict will be resolved. Stories with little or no conflict are dull and slow-moving, and inspire readers to say that nothing happened in the book. Conversely, stories with nothing but conflict seem shallow and contrived. Most formula series fiction, for example, is heavy on conflict, light on character.

To build a plot, an author places the main character *(protagonist)* in situations in which she comes into conflict with something or someone else *(antagonist)*. The antagonist might be another character, nature, society, or self. A great many children's novels center on **character vs. character** conflict, from the stories about facing up to the bully down the street to those about adjusting to life with a new stepparent. In *Jacob Have I Loved* (Crowell, 1980),

Katherine Paterson explored this sort of conflict in depth by placing her protagonist, Louise, in a constant struggle against her twin sister, Caroline, about whom she felt intense jealousy and resentment. **Character vs. nature** has been popularized in survival stories, such as *Hatchet* (Bradbury, 1987) by Gary Paulsen, in which a young teenage boy struggles to survive alone in the wilderness after a plane crash. These two types of conflict are by far the most common in children's novels aimed at eight- to eleven-year-olds, most likely because they detail the type of outward struggles with which children can easily identify.

Character vs. society need not involve conflict with society at large; instead it may be society in microcosm, viewed on a child's scale, such as the society of a neighborhood or school. Walter Dean Myers develops this sort of conflict to show the complexity of peer pressure and identity among urban youth in *Scorpions* (Harper, 1988). Rachel Vail also deals unflinchingly with peer pressure among suburban girls at summer camp in *Daring to Be Abigail* (Orchard, 1996), but develops the conflict as **character vs. self**: Because Abigail is so desperate to fit in with the crowd, she is willing to risk losing her individual identity and sense of self in the process.

PLOT DEVELOPMENT

Conflict can be used in different ways to build different types of plots. An **episodic** plot is made up of a series of conflicts that are introduced and resolved, usually chapter by chapter. Episodic plots are generally easier for newly independent readers, who often have difficulty sustaining concentration when they first begin to read chapter books. Beverly Cleary's popular books about Henry Huggins, Beezus, and Ramona are perfect for this level, largely due to their episodic plots.

In a **progressive** plot, conflict is introduced early in the book and carried through until there is a climax and resolution near the story's end. Progressive plots generally follow the same general pattern of action:

1) Presentation of brief background that sets the stage
2) Introduction of conflict
3) Development of conflict
4) Climax or turning point
5) Resolution

In children's novels the conflict is usually introduced very early on: Something happens to grab the reader's attention, to arouse curiosity, to entice the child to read on. After briefly setting the scene as Copenhagen in World War II, Lois Lowry introduces the conflict on page two of *Number the Stars* (Houghton, 1989) when the main characters, racing each other home from school, are stopped by German soldiers.

The development of conflict is an essential part of the plot, since it accounts for most of a novel. It must be well paced so that the story doesn't lag, and it must continually stimulate the reader's interest. An author can achieve this by using two devices: **suspense** and **foreshadowing**.

Suspense raises questions into the reader's mind: What

will happen next? Why did the character do that? When the girls come up against the German soldiers in *Number the Stars*, for example, we immediately wonder: Why would soldiers stop a group of little girls? Have they done something wrong? Are the soldiers friends or enemies? We keep reading to find out. Suspense that occurs at the end of a chapter is referred to as a **cliffhanger**, and it propels readers directly on into the next chapter so that they can find out what happens.

Foreshadowing gives us clues as to what will happen later in the story. To use the same example from *Number the Stars*, two instances of foreshadowing occur in the scene with the soldiers. We note that one of the girls, Ellen, finds the experience much more frightening than her friend Annemarie does. We will later learn that Ellen is Jewish. Annemarie's little sister, Kirsti, on the other hand, pushes one soldier's hand away and says, *"Don't!"* when he strokes her hair. This foreshadows the acts of resistance we will see later on in the book. Foreshadowing builds anticipation, causing readers to make predictions about what will happen later in the story.

When foreshadowing is obvious and frequent, the plot is said to be predictable. In general, children seem far less troubled by predictable plots than adults. Many children express delight at figuring out a book's ending on their own — and then they'll turn around and read the whole thing over again, just to bask awhile in their own cleverness.

A good example of less obvious foreshadowing is present in the opening scene from *Number the Stars* as well: Annemarie encounters German soldiers once again at the end of the book, and she survives by behaving as her little sister, Kristi, did in the first encounter. Subtle uses of fore-shadowing give readers a sense that the ending was inevitable, even if they did not guess the outcome earlier in the story. Experienced readers usually find this sort of ending more satisfying.

And what about that ending? After a steady buildup of suspense and foreshadowing, the protagonist ultimately engages in some sort of final confrontation with the antag-onist, which will lead to a turning point in the conflict and a resolution. In children's novels the protagonist almost always wins the battle against the antagonist. To return once again to *Number the Stars*, the final confrontation occurs when Annemarie carries a basket containing some-thing of utmost importance to her uncle in the Resistance movement and is stopped by German soldiers. By pre-tending to be a silly little girl carrying lunch to her uncle, she outwits the soldiers and manages to get the important information to her uncle so that he can help her friend Ellen escape to Sweden. Two chapters follow this climactic scene and give a final resolution to the story, so that readers feel a sense of satisfaction and completeness. Occasionally, a children's novel will leave matters unresolved in an **open ending** by suggesting two or more possible interpretations and leaving it up to the reader to decide what happened.

Novels for children sometimes use more complex structures than a straightforward progressive or epi-sodic plot. A **parallel** structure builds two progressive plots simultaneously. Sharon Creech skillfully developed parallel plots in *Walk Two Moons* by embedding the story of Sal's friend Phoebe into Sal's own story. Elements in the story of Phoebe's mother's disappearance subtly foreshadow events in Sal's search for her own missing mother. Creech makes this otherwise complex structure straightforward for young readers because she clearly delineates the progression of one plot by limiting its action to a seven-day cross-country trip from Ohio to Lewiston, Idaho. As a result, readers know exactly where they are at every point in the story.

Another possible structure in children's fiction combines a progressive main plot with subplots. In *The Ear, the Eye and the Arm* (Orchard, 1994) Nancy Farmer builds a main plot around the actions of three siblings kidnaped and lost in twenty-second-century Harare, Zimbabwe, interwoven with two secondary plots involving the people who are searching for them. The subplots, in this case, are episodic, which makes the complex structure a bit easier to follow.

When you evaluate the plot of any children's novel, think of it from several angles. What kind of narrative order does it have? Will this order be clear for the intended audience? If the author chose a more complex type of order, what purpose does it serve? How does it illuminate character or advance the plot? What kind of conflict do you notice in the story? Is there too much or not enough conflict present? How is the conflict used to build the plot? What type of plot structure is used? Is it appropriate for the intended audience? If the plot structure is more complex, how does the author clarify the ordering of events for young readers? Do you notice clear instances of suspense and foreshadowing? How is conflict resolved in the story? Does the resolution seem credible?

CHARACTERIZATION

The *characters* are a crucial part of any children's novel, because they serve as a link between the reader and the story. The link is established when the child reader is able to identify with the actions, motives, and feelings of the main character in a story. One way for the author to accomplish this is to choose a main character who is close to the same age as readers in the book's target audience. A book aimed at nine- to eleven-year-olds, for instance, is less likely to succeed if its protagonist is only six years old. On the other hand, children do like to identify with characters who are a couple of years older than they are, so a book aimed at nine- to eleven-year-olds works well with a thirteen-year-old protagonist.

TYPES OF CHARACTERS

Authors can also establish identity between the protagonist and the reader by creating a main character who seems realistic and believable. Through *character development* the author reveals complexity by showing us how characters think, act, and feel, so that readers get a sense of a real, three-dimensional person. Not all characters in a story need to be equally well developed for the novel to succeed as good fiction.

Secondary characters play smaller roles and often serve a different purpose, such as to advance the plot. They are usually defined by one or two characteristics alone and therefore seem to be one-dimensional or *flat.* Sometimes these characteristics are immediately recognizable because we've seen them countless times in other books and on television. Those created in this way are called *stock characters.* The pirate with an eye patch and a peg leg is one example of a stock character, and the smart, prissy girl who is the teacher's pet is another. When the characteristics have their basis in a recognized cultural or social shorthand, the stock characters are said to be *stereotyped.* We see this in such stock characters as the black kid who's good in basketball or the Asian-American kid who's good in math. While an author might succeed in making a case for traits of this sort in a fully developed character, the use of them as defining characteristics for secondary characters is an indication of laziness — or even bias, conscious or otherwise — on the part of the author.

Primary characters are those who are closer to the central conflict in the story, and since they play a larger role, we expect a higher degree of character development. We refer to well-developed characters as *rounded* and those who grow and change over the course of a novel as *dynamic.* Since most children's novels feature child characters who experience some degree of maturation as a result of the conflict they face, we expect good fiction to have a dynamic, rounded main character.

CHARACTER DEVELOPMENT

We come to know characters by observing them in several different ways: how they look, what they do, what they think, what they say, and how they are viewed by other characters in the novel. Throughout the course of a novel an author reveals complexities of character through *appearance, action, thought,* and *dialogue.* A well-rounded character is developed using a combination of all of these devices. I will cite some examples of how this is done, using the main character in Karen Cushman's *The Midwife's Apprentice* to demonstrate.

Readers build mental images of characters based on what the author tells us about a character's **appearance**. As a surface quality, it is often the defining characteristic in a secondary character, but it it rarely definitive in a rounded primary character. An author can use a description of appearance to arouse a reader's curiosity about a character initially, however, as Cushman does when she introduces us to the main character in *The Midwife's Apprentice*: "How old she was was hard to say. She was small and pale, with the frightened air of an ill-used child, but her scrawny underfed body did give off a hint of woman. . . ." This description of Beetle's appearance gives us a sense of the sort of life she has led that helps to set the stage for the novel.

Actions are also visible only on the surface, but they provide more insight into character because they spring from internal thoughts and motives. While many actions in a novel serve to move the plot along, some exist only to reveal character. Note, for example, what the following description of action tells us about Beetle's character:

> *Once she found a nest of baby mice who had frozen in the cold, and she left them by the fence post for the cat. But her heart ached when she thought of the tiny hairless bodies in those strong jaws, so she buried them deep in the dung heap and left the cat to do his own hunting.*

The author can enter directly into the main character's mind to reveal aspects of character through **thought**. Returning home from the Saint Swithin's Day Fair, Beetle is mistaken for a girl named Alyce when a stranger thrusts a piece of paper in front of her face and asks her to read it. The chance encounter has an enormous impact on the girl's self-concept, as is revealed to us when she asks herself, "Did she then look like someone who could read?" On the spot, she decides to take the name Alyce for herself, and we learn not only how this came to be but why: "Alyce sounded clean and friendly and smart. You could love someone named Alyce."

Note how skillfully Cushman used this device by restricting Beetle's thoughts to the name Alyce itself, rather than launching into lengthy self-examination and soul-searching that would have been out of character for her. One of the most common traps that writers for children fall into is that of putting their own thoughts into the heads of young characters, thus giving them a wisdom beyond their age and experience.

In the subsequent chapter, we see Beetle, now Alyce, assert her newly established self-confidence through **dialogue** as she insists people call her Alyce, even in the face of ridicule and, in one case, danger, as when she is threatened by a gang of drunken village boys:

> *"Dung Beetle, give me a kiss," called the boy with red hair.*
> *"Alyce," whispered Beetle, surrounded by boys and abandoned by the cat.*

Just one word, whispered in a carefully constructed context, demonstrates the extent of the girl's determination to establish a new identity.

In addition to developing Beetle's character through her own actions, thoughts, and speech, Cushman adds depth and humor to the characterization by showing her to us through the eyes of other characters, who continually make comments about the girl. Early on, in fact, she is largely characterized by these impressions of others, right down to her very name: Dung Beetle. Through the **comments of others** an author can add further dimension to characters by showing us how they fit (or don't fit) into the social life surrounding them. Direct **comments of the author** can also be used for this purpose. Both must be used with care, however, or we end up with a less satisfying characterization that is based on telling, rather than showing, what a character is like.

All these factors must be taken into consideration when we evaluate characterization in fiction. What types of characters do you identify in the book? Are they realistic and believable? Is the main character dynamic? What devices does the author use to develop the main character? What kinds of changes do the characters undergo? How are secondary characters developed? What purposes do the secondary characters serve? How do events that occur in the novel shape the characters?

POINT OF VIEW

When authors create fictional worlds, they choose a particular stance within that world that defines what its perimeters will be. This is determined by *point of view,* the vantage point from which the action in the story is viewed and related. The author may choose to tell the story from inside a character's head or by looking over a character's shoulder or by viewing the entire scene from a distance. Each of these choices offers different advantages, challenges, and limitations.

First person point of view tells a story from inside the character's head. It is readily identifiable due to the use of the pronoun "I" by the narrator. First person has the advantage of evoking a powerful sense of reality through the immediacy of the character's voice. This strength is also its greatest limitation: The narrative is limited to what the main character thinks, observes, or hears from another character. Some authors try to get around this limitation by using dialogue in which one character "briefs" the protagonist to get information across to the reader. Overuse of this device may be an indication that the author has not mastered first person.

An **omniscient** point of view allows for much greater freedom and flexibility, in that the author can move around inside the story and enter into the thoughts and feelings of any of the characters. The disadvantage is that it can make the story more difficult for young readers to follow, as they often have difficulty following transitions from one character to the next. A *limited omniscient* point of view, in which the author uses third person but sticks to the viewpoint of one character, is easier for young readers to comprehend.

An **objective** point of view uses third person but does not enter into the mind of a character at all. Rather, action is described completely from outside observations. This point of view is used effectively in realistic animal stories that dramatize action in the natural world. It becomes more challenging when used with human characters, however, because it requires readers to make their own connections between explicit actions and implicit emotions.

Children's authors sometimes bring together multiple points of view to construct a distinctive narrative. In *Bull Run* (Harper, 1993) Paul Fleischman used sixteen points of view to build a patchwork of history in a fictional account of the Civil War battle. In *Nothing but the Truth: A Documentary Novel* (Orchard, 1991) Avi employs dialogues, diary entries, memos, letters, and transcripts to build an unusual objective point of view from which readers must draw their own conclusions. In both of these novels, the idea of point of view becomes the theme.

Whichever point of view an author chooses, he should remain consistent throughout. If he chooses to tell a story in first person from the point of view of an eleven-year-old main character, he must stay with it. He cannot enter the mind of the character's mother or best friend or tell us things that the character hasn't experienced. When you evaluate point of view, keep the following question in mind: Who is the narrator of the story, and what is this narrator likely to know?

SETTING

Setting in a novel can function either as a **backdrop** or as an **integral** part of the story. As the name suggests, backdrop settings are created from vivid descriptive details that may be interesting in and of themselves, but the story could easily be moved to another setting without losing much. Lois Lowry's series of books about Anastasia Krupnik, for example, could be set in any middle-class American neighborhood. They draw their power from plot and characters, not from their setting.

Other novels would disintegrate if they were removed from their settings, because setting is integral to the action and characters. This is especially true of historical novels, in which setting often functions to clarify the conflict in the story, as happens in Lois Lowry's *Number the Stars*. An integral setting must be clearly described and made as real as the characters, so that the reader can not only picture it but feel it.

Aside from **clarifying conflict**, integral settings function in several ways. The setting can act as an **antagonist**, as it invariably does in survival stories since the protagonist is always at the mercy of threats from the environment. In *The Ear, the Eye and the Arm*, Nancy Farmer developed four separate distinctive settings as antagonistic in her exploration of the difficulties of fitting in.

Settings frequently serve to **illuminate character**. In her sequence of books about the Logan family, Mildred D. Taylor has created the fictional Depression-era small town of Strawberry, Mississippi, to explore race relations and to show the strength and dignity of the African-American family.

Setting can also operate on a **symbolic** level by encompassing two levels of meaning simultaneously. In *Walk Two Moons* by Sharon Creech, the setting on the road functions in this way, in that the long stretch of highway represents both the literal and symbolic distance between Sal and her mother. As the car edges closer to Lewiston, Idaho, so too does Sal come closer to an acceptance of her mother's departure.

STYLE

Language dictates style in all writing. With respect to fiction, we look at both the literal and metaphorical ways an author uses language. What words has the author chosen, and how have they been put together? **Literary devices** enrich the language of the novel and evoke emotional responses in the reader. Authors of children's fiction face a special challenge, as they write for an audience with limited experiences when it comes to understanding the symbolic use of language. Outstanding children's fiction uses literary devices geared directly toward young readers.

In *Words of Stone* Kevin Henkes uses a remarkable range of literary devices, all based on a child's worldview. His prose is filled with **connotations** related to sensual childhood observations of people and the natural world of the backyard, making his metaphorical use of language easily understandable to child readers. I will use examples from *Words of Stone* to define the various types of literary devices.

Imagery is the use of words that appeal to any of the senses: sight, smell, sound, taste, and touch. *Words of Stone* is filled with child-friendly imagery: Blaze states that Joselle lives in "a house the color of celery." He notes that she "smelled dusty, like a ladybug," and he makes a reference to his own "blister-smooth skin."

Figurative language refers to the use of words in a non-literal way. There are numerous examples of figurative language in *Words of Stone*, beginning with the title itself, which signifies the difficulty Blaze has in communicating with his father as well as Joselle's tendency to build walls between herself and others by lying. A common type of figurative language is *personification,* which is investing non-human objects or animals with human characteristics. Henkes uses personification when Blaze's father tosses a key across the breakfast table and it "stopped right beside

Blaze's plate, kissing his fork." *Simile*, the comparison of two dissimilar things, generally with the words "like" or "as," is another common type of figurative language we see throughout the book. After he spends a day playing outside, "dirt stuck to Blaze's sweaty body like bread crumbs," and when he speaks to Joselle, his voice is "as quiet as insects' wings." *Metaphors* make implied comparisons. Henkes uses stones metaphorically throughout the novel on several different levels. These objects for serious outdoor play used by both Blaze and Joselle—by Blaze to mark the graves of his imaginary friends, and by Joselle to spell out mean-spirited messages to Blaze—are linked by implication to the stone on Blaze's mother's grave. Once Blaze and Joselle resolve their differences, he observes that "the stones were white moons that bled together."

Hyperbole, the use of exaggeration, characterizes the the speech of melodramatic Joselle: "For the first couple years of your life, you were probably no bigger than a salt shaker. . . . I'll bet your parents have photographs from when you were three, but they tell you they were from the day you were born." By way of contrast, Blaze is often characterized with **understatement** to underscore his timid nature: "Blaze didn't like spiders particularly, except from a distance."

Kevin Henkes also uses **sound** devices to enrich the language of his novels. Some examples:

Alliteration: the repetition of initial consonants, as we see with both *s* and *l* in the phrase "legs scissoring the sunlight," which imitates the sound of scissors cutting.

Assonance: the repetition of similar vowel sounds.

"Puddles dotted Floy's lawn like scattered mirrors." The long vowel sounds in the first four words come in quick succession like dripping water.

Consonance: the close repetition of consonant sounds. Note the repetition of the fluttering *l* sound when Joselle's grandmother tells her: "Your eyelids are the color of my needlepoint lilacs."

Onomatopoeia: the use of words that sound like their meanings. We see an example of this when Blaze's father allows him to help attach canvas to frames. "The staple gun had a nasty little kick that jolted Blaze's arm, and it made a whooshing noise that reminded Blaze of getting a vaccination."

Rhythm: the pattern of words in a sentence that gives it a particular flow, or *cadence.* Note the way in which Henkes uses rhythm in the following sentence to give readers a playful sense of somersaulting downhill: "Summer afternoons on the hill smelled of heat and dirt and grass and weeds and laziness."

Allusion is reference to literature or historical events that are part of our common cultural heritage. It is less frequently used as a device in children's books simply because children typically do not have the necessary background for recognizing and appreciating it. It is not, however, unheard of. Lois Lowry provides a stunning example of literary allusion in *Number the Stars* when Annemarie's courageous journey through the forest to take the basket to her uncle clearly echoes the story of "Little Red Riding Hood." Even though this is a folktale that most children know well, they might not expect it to show up in a novel. For this reason Lowry draws a clear connection to it earlier in the novel with a scene in which Annemarie tells the story to her younger sister at bedtime.

Diction is another aspect of an author's style that enriches the manner in which a story is told. Sometimes referred to as the author's *voice*, diction injects prose with the flavor of a particular time and place by using words and grammatical structures native to the story's setting and characters. Diction can appear as distinctive in both dialogue and narrative. With dialogue an author uses diction to approximate the way spoken language sounds. With narrative diction creates a sense of the story as the characters who live in it might tell it themselves.

Virginia Hamilton is a master of diction in all her literary works. Her writing reflects the varied uses of black English in different times and places, as well as among different ages and classes of African Americans. Note her use of diction in both narrative and speech in the following passage from *Sweet Whispers, Brother Rush* (Philomel, 1982), as her main character, Tree, makes her way home from school:

> *She was holding her books tight to her chest, hiding herself from the dudes. She had begun growing into a woman, which was the reason the dudes had started to catcall her:*
>
> *"Hey, little girl, when you going to let me take you* out *?"*

*"Sweet Tree, I'll walk you home,
bay-buh. Do Dab know you walkin
by these shifless clowns alone? Do
your brother leave you in the house
by you-sef?"*

Compare this with the language she uses in *The Magical Adventures of Pretty Pearl* (Harper, 1983), set in the South during the Reconstruction era:

Dwahro held his head high with pride. While other folks might sit in pity's chair, Dwahro's patent leather shoes alone made him look like he was at least sitting there stirring a pot of luck. Mother Pearl had breathed on his shoes and made them shine like new money.

"Folk gone be down in sorrow's kitchen, you wait and see," said Mother Pearl. "We gone have our work and play all laid out in de skillet and already fryin'."

Tone is the reflection of the author's attitude toward the story. It corresponds to the tone of voice in spoken language; however, since we can't hear a tone of voice in writing, the author conveys this sense through style. The tone in a children's novel may be humorous, as it is in *The*

Midwife's Apprentice, or serious, as it is in *Number the Stars*. In both of these examples, the tone gives us an idea of how the author feels about the story.

In children's books we sometimes see instances of a condescending tone, which indicates that the author believes her ideas are really too complex for children to understand, so she must simplify it for them by explaining everything or trying to make it cute. We see, even more frequently, books with a sentimental tone. The latter often implies that the author believes all the world's great problems could be easily solved if they were viewed through the innocent eyes of a child. Other times a sentimental tone reveals that the author is fascinated with his own childhood but cares very little about the childhood of others, namely his readers.

To evaluate style, look at the ways in which an author uses language. Do you notice a distinctive style? How does the story sound when it is read aloud? What literary devices do you notice? How do these relate to the reality of child readers?

THEME

Theme can be one of the most elusive aspects of fiction, but it is an important one, because it answers the question: What is the story about? When you ask children this question, you often get a recitation of plot details in response. But theme is more than what happened in a story. Theme reflects the overall idea the author was trying to get across to readers in the first place. The fact that a child has difficulty articulating this deeper meaning doesn't necessarily mean that the theme wasn't understood.

All the pieces of a work of fiction—plot, characters, point of view, setting, and style—add up to its theme; that is, a significant, underlying truth embedded just beneath the surface of the story. If you, as an adult reader, have difficulty determining what, exactly, the theme of the book is, it may be an indication that the author did not have a clear theme in mind to start with or was unsuccessful in getting the idea across to readers through the story as it now stands. Conversely, many books are easily summed up in a phrase, which may suggest that the author did not succeed in combining fictional elements to give depth to the story.

When we examine theme in a work of children's fiction, it is important for us, as adults, to keep in mind that children are new to the idea of "significant truth." A truth that is commonplace to an experienced adult reader may be a real eye-opener for a child, particularly if the child is given the opportunity to discover meaning on his or her own. The thrill of discovery is the great promise a book holds for a reader.

In many outstanding works of fiction, the underlying truth, or theme, is left open to interpretation. The author sets the stage for discovery, but individual readers must be trusted to bring their own experiences to the reading of any book. When an author succeeds in a writing a gripping story with a fresh style, peopled with characters who seem real and alive, her work is completed. The rest she leaves in the hands of the readers.

Writing a Review

hildren's book reviewing has had a long, rich history in the United States. In his landmark study *The Rise of Children's Book Reviewing in America, 1865–1881* (Bowker, 1968), Richard L. Darling found that children's books were regularly reviewed in mid- to late-nineteenth-century literary monthlies and popular magazines by reviewers who showed a considerable understanding of children and their books. More than one hundred years later this sort of understanding continues to play a crucial role in children's book reviewing. Then, as now, the function of reviews appearing in the popular press was to call new books to the attention of potential readers, or, as Virginia Woolf succinctly described it: "partly to sort current literature; partly to advertise the author; partly to inform the public." This attention to new children's books in general periodical literature was carried well into the twentieth century, with regular children's book review columns appearing in publications such as the *New York Herald Tribune, The New York Times Book Review,* the *Chicago Tribune,* and *The Saturday Review of Literature.*

With the development of children's library services in the early twentieth century, reviewing began to serve another function: to provide children's librarians with a guide for selecting books. *Booklist,* a professional library journal published by the American Library Association and consisting solely of reviews of new titles recommended for purchase, has included a children's books section since its inception in 1905. Other general library periodicals, such as *Kirkus Reviews* and *Library Journal,* included children's book reviews as well. *The Horn Book* magazine, founded in 1924 by Bertha Mahony Miller and Elinor Whitney Field, was entirely devoted to articles about and reviews of children's books and throughout much of the twentieth century was very influential in setting contemporary standards for excellence in children's books. In 1954 the children's book section of *Library Journal* broke off to establish its own publication, now called *School Library Journal,* which strives to review every book published for children whether it is recommended for purchase or not. At the University of Chicago the *Bulletin of the Center for Children's Books* was established in 1945; it remains the only national journal to consist entirely of children's book reviews. Taken as a whole, these five journals (*Booklist, Bulletin of the Center for Children's Books, Horn Book, Kirkus,* and *School Library Journal*) comprise the basis for most school and public library book selection in the United States.

Many school and public library systems have created their own internal review processes that may require librarians to prepare written or oral reviews of newly published books being considered for purchase. Others use group discussion as a means of evaluating books and sharpening critical skills. At the very least, children's librarians read a wide selection of reviews from the professional review journals listed above in order to make decisions about which books to purchase for the library collection. While some purchase decisions can be made quickly based on popular demand or professional wisdom, most selections are made with a great deal of care and deliberation based, in whole or in part, on reviews. The reviewer, then, owes it to her audience to use care and deliberation in preparing a review.

THE DISTINCTION BETWEEN REVIEWING AND LITERARY CRITICISM

Although the words "review" and "criticism" are often used interchangeably, most experts differentiate between the two by pointing out that reviews are limited by time and space; that is, a review is published as close as possible to the publication date of the book under consideration, and the reviewer is generally limited to a set number of words.

In an eloquent essay entitled "Out on a Limb with the Critics: Some Random Thoughts on the Present State of the Criticism of Children's Literature," Paul Heins, former editor of *The Horn Book*, drew the following distinction: "Reviewing . . . is only concerned with what is imminent in publishing, with what is being produced at the present time; and does its job well by selecting, classifying, and evaluating—evaluating for the time being. Criticism deals with literature in perspective and places a book in a larger context. . . ."

This is not to say that criticism should not enter into reviewing. In fact, Heins makes the point in the same article that it would be virtually impossible to keep criticism out of a review: "Any form of literary classification, comparison, or evaluation must also be considered a form of criticism."

PREPARING TO REVIEW

Because the reviewer does not have the advantage of time, it is to her advantage to have a broad knowledge of contemporary children's literature as a context for "selecting, classifying, and evaluating." A solid background in the literature also helps the reviewer put the book into a context so that she can answer the questions: Are there other books like this one? If so, how does it compare to them? What does it offer that is unique?

SELECTING BOOKS TO REVIEW

When you write reviews for a professional journal or as part of an internal review process, chances are you will not have a choice about which books you will review, since they will most likely be assigned to you. These assignments may be made in accordance with your own particular areas of interest or expertise; however, if you are given a book about which you simply cannot be objective, return it so that it can be assigned to another reviewer who can give it a fair review. Part of any book review editor's job is to match books with reviewers, and she will no doubt appreciate your honesty if you feel you are not the right reviewer for the book. Since objectivity is an important part of every reviewer's approach, it is better not to review books written by personal friends (or enemies) and to avoid reviewing books that give you a chance to air a complaint or grind an ax.

If you are reviewing for a general publication, such as your local newspaper, you may have the opportunity to choose the books you will review. There are no hard-and-fast rules about what to select, but it is best to choose a book that is current, readily available, and likely to be of interest to the audience for whom you are writing. It may be the latest book by a well-known popular writer or a first book from a promising newcomer. You may choose a book to fit the current season (a great new biography about George Washington for Presidents' Day, for example), a title that can be linked with a current news event, or one that you know will be of local interest. When you can articulate exactly why you have chosen to review one particular book over all the others at this particular time, you have already begun to write an opening sentence that will link the book to your audience.

READING AND NOTE TAKING

A reviewer's first obligation is to give a book a thorough and careful reading. There are, of course, different ways to approach this task. In her study of children's book reviewers, Kathleen W. Craver found that some reviewers prefer to read a book all the way through, jotting down an occasional note along the way, and then return for a second reading to make more detailed notes. Others take careful notes during their initial reading and read straight through the second time around to get a better sense of the author's style and pacing.

Before you begin to read, try to place the book in its broad category by type or genre: Is it nonfiction, a folktale, a transitional book? Usually (but not always) the classification is fairly straightforward. Once you have determined the category, you can use the corresponding chapter in *From Cover to Cover* as your framework for evaluation. As you read, you may jot down notes to outline the book's structure or the main developments in the plot; to respond to questions you ask yourself as part of the critical process; and to keep track of questions the book under review raises in your mind. These questions may require you to consult outside sources before you begin to write a review.

According to Craver's study, some reviewers write the review immediately after the second reading and some take up to a week to mull things over before beginning to write. Regardless of their approach, all the reviewers cited rereading and note taking as an essential part of the review process.

CONSULTING OUTSIDE SOURCES

Many of the reviewers who took part in Craver's study also indicated that they frequently sought outside information to assist them with a review. This generally consisted of discussing the book with a colleague or reading it aloud to a group of children to get their responses. It is not considered "cheating" to ask others for their opinion of a book you are reviewing. In fact, if you have kept an open mind toward the book, the responses of others can greatly enrich your critical perspective.

Many critics find it especially helpful to get responses from actual children. If there is an easy and natural way for you to do this, such as sharing a picture book with preschoolers during a regular library storytime, by all means take advantage of the opportunity. But use the experience as one aspect of your critical approach, not the be-all and end-all of your assessment. And please, never allow your review to sink into a description of your three-year-old daughter's response to the book. Because your relationship to the child is of a personal, rather than professional, nature, this is not only irrelevant and unprofessional, it is self-indulgent. Save it for your annual holiday form letter.

In the course of your note taking, if you jotted down any questions that require some outside fact checking, this is the time to do it. When you are reviewing a nonfiction book, you may want to consult other books on the same subject for comparison. This will not only broaden your own background knowledge of the subject itself, it will help you think about the book you are reviewing in contrast to other books for children on the same subject. You can mention related children's books in your review to compare and contrast the new book to others that are available. Librarians, in particular, appreciate these sorts of critical insights; however, it is important that you don't allow yourself to get carried away. Your primary responsibility is to review one book, not to write about every book that has been published to date on the same subject.

We have all had the experience of reading a work of fiction in which certain historical, regional, or cultural details just don't ring true. This can raise questions such as: Would it have been likely for a nineteenth-century Amish family to join a wagon train? Did the Iroquois live in tipis? Is the black English an author uses in dialogue accurate? You may want to follow up on some of these questions, especially if they are essential parts of the book. Using the question about the Amish family as an example: If the family itself is the central focus of the book and their joining the wagon train a major factor in the plot, it would be important for you to do some background research to answer the question. If they are merely mentioned briefly in one paragraph in chapter 4, you may not want to spend a lot of time pursuing it.

Occasionally, reviewers seek the opinions of content specialists to help determine the accuracy or authenticity of a book that raises questions. If you suspect there is a problem with a book that claims one can avoid contracting AIDS by showering after unprotected sex, for example,

you can double-check the facts with a local expert to con-
firm your suspicions. If you do consult a content specialist,
remember that while a content specialist is an expert in her
particular field and is able to evaluate the accuracy of *what*
information is provided, you are the expert when it comes
to *how* this information is presented in a book for children.

WHAT TO INCLUDE IN A BIBLIOGRAPHIC CITATION

All reviews must open with a bibliographic citation
that includes details such as author, title, and publisher.
Although reviewers have many choices to make con-
cerning the content of their reviews, bibliographic citations are fairly standard.

Reviews that are published in general publications,
such as newspapers and popular magazines, typically
include only a brief heading that includes title (including
subtitle), author, illustrator (if any), publisher, price, and
sometimes the year of publication and number of pages.
Every publication has its own in-house format for citations—check a back issue if the editor hasn't given you a
style sheet, and include all the same information in the
order shown. You will need to include a complete citation
at the head of your review. A standard style for citations
appearing in general publication is:

Sees Behind Trees. By Michael Dorris. Hyperion,
1996. 96 pages. $14.95

FOR AN ILLUSTRATED BOOK:

Monday's Troll. By Jack Prelutsky. Illustrated by
Peter Sís. Greenwillow, 1996. 39 pages. $16.00

Since reviews that appear in professional review journals are used for book selection, the bibliographic citations
are more detailed and always include the International
Standard Book Number (ISBN) for both the trade and
library binding. In addition, they also may include the
Library of Congress (LC) number, publication date, and
an indication as to whether the book was reviewed from
galleys. The reviews themselves are generally arranged by
the last name of the author, and that information appears
first in bibliographic citations in review journals. Every
journal's style for citing bibliographic information varies
slightly, but for the most part all reviews contain the same
information:

Dorris, Michael. *Sees Behind Trees.* Hyperion,
    1996. 96 pages. Tr. $14.95 ISBN 0-7868-0224-3;
    PLB $14.89 ISBN 0-7868-2215-5

FOR AN ILLUSTRATED BOOK:

Prelutsky, Jack. *Monday's Troll.* Illustrated by
    Peter Sís. Greenwillow, 1996. 39 pages.
    Tr. $16.00 ISBN 0-688-09644-1); PLB $15.93
    ISBN 0-688-14373-3

In all professional journals and in many popular publications, reviewers are expected to indicate an age range for the book's target audience, either in the bibliographic data or in the body of the review. This judgment should be based on your own knowledge of children's responses to literature and your assessment of the book itself, not the ages suggested by the publisher on the jacket flap. If your assessment differs markedly from the publisher's recommendation, it may be worth mentioning in the review.

WRITING THE REVIEW

Once you have done all the necessary reading, note taking, and fact checking, you are ready to begin writing the actual review. A good review will briefly describe the contents, scope, and style of a book; critically assess its quality; and suggest its potential audience. Phyllis K. Kennemer has labeled these categories *descriptive, analytical,* and *sociological.* She gives the following examples to illustrate:

> **Descriptive:** Objective statements about the characters, plot, theme, or illustrations.
> **Analytical:** Statements about literary and artistic elements, including evaluation, comparison, and mention of contributions to the field.
> **Sociological:** Judgments based on nonliterary considerations, such as potential controversial elements or predictions about popularity.

One of the most common criticisms of children's book reviews today is that they rely heavily on description and include very little in the way of analysis. As you begin to sketch out your review, it may be helpful to think about your responses in terms of these categories, as you will want to include each type of statement in your review. As a way of getting started, divide a piece of scratch paper into three sections and label them *descriptive, analytical,* and *sociological.* Using your notes, make up a list of all the points you would like to include in your review, placing each one in its corresponding category. If the descriptive side of your paper seems to be filling up rapidly and there is very little in the analytical or sociological category to balance it, try using the descriptive points listed as a springboard for critical thinking by asking yourself questions about them. If you have noted, for example, that the book is illustrated with color photographs, ask yourself how they support the text. Are they well placed? Do they have clear captions? What sorts of things do they show?

DECIDING WHAT TO INCLUDE

Because reviews are generally brief (100–400 words, with an average length of 150 words in children's book review journals), you will obviously not be able to include all your points, so you will have to decide which ones are the most important. Consider these questions: Which points relate to the book as a whole? Which ones will give readers a sense of the book's style or unique qualities? Which ones best support your overall objective assessment of the book? How do they contribute to a fair, balanced judgment about the book?

Children's book reviewers are sometimes taken to task by readers who order a book based on positive reviews, only to find that one of the characters uses profanity on page 43. "Why didn't you mention that in the review?" the readers ask, accusing the reviewer of misleading them. Book review editor Betsy Hearne discusses this issue at length in her essay "A Reviewer's Story," concluding that as a reviewer, she opts to mention potentially controversial elements "only if they warrant analysis as an important aspect of the work. Anything more would serve as a censor signal to steer librarians away from dangerous books and focus attention on didactic evaluation."

Critic Zena Sutherland discusses the choices a reviewer must make when it comes to pointing out minor errors and discrepancies: "In a review, a negative comment can loom deceptively large and mislead the reader. If, for example, [a] pictorial discrepancy is minor, one doesn't want readers to assume that the illustrations are replete with inaccuracies." Again, as Hearne stresses above, the mention of such details must be weighed against their significance to the book as a whole.

As you make decisions about what points to include in your review, you can also begin to think about how you will organize them. How do they relate to each other? Is there a logical order that emerges as you look at them together?

Does one important element stand out as a central point in your evaluation? Can it be used as a thesis statement to open your review? Or will you start with a descriptive statement and then move on to your analytical points?

WRITING IT ALL DOWN

The opening sentence is important because it sets the tone for your entire review. Chosen with care, it can enliven your review and give it a logical structure that makes it easier for you to write and for others to read.

If you are writing for a general audience, you need to grab your readers' attention with the opening sentence. You may also need to provide a bit of context for them, since you can't assume that they know anything at all about children's books. Finding a hook that quickly links your audience with children's literature in general and the book you're reviewing specifically is an effective way to open a review for general readers:

> *With his popular, innovative books such as* The Way Things Work *(Houghton, 1988) and the Caldecott Award–winner* Black and White *(Houghton, 1990), David Macaulay has established himself as a master at producing books in which words and pictures work together to create a story that must be completed in the reader's imagination.*

When I wrote this opening sentence in a review of David Macaulay's *Shortcut* (Houghton, 1995) for the *Milwaukee Journal Sentinel,* I consciously used a reference to the Caldecott Medal because I assumed that most adult readers would recognize it as significant, even if they had never heard of David Macaulay. I also used the adjectives "popular" and "innovative" to describe his books not only because they are appropriate but because I thought they would be likely to pique a general reader's interest. I wanted to make the casual reader stop and think: "Hmmm, what sort of books are popular with kids today? What is considered innovative?"

One of the first things readers see when they look at a review is the title of the book. You may want to open a review by making some reference to the title, particularly if it is intriguingly unusual. Roger Sutton does this effectively in his *Bulletin of the Center for Children's Books* review of Nina Bawden's *Granny the Pag* (Clarion, 1996):

> *Cat calls her grandmother "The Pag" in affectionate remembrance of a childhood tantrum in which she misspelled a sign meant to read* Granny is a Pig.

Sutton's selection of this particular detail gives readers quick insight into Cat's character and gives us a sense of her relationship with her grandmother, in addition to explaining the book's odd title.

The vast majority of reviews in professional journals

begin with a descriptive account of the book itself. These need not be dry summations, however. Notice how effectively Ilene Cooper uses this technique to echo the book's tone and entice readers in her *Booklist* review of Anne Fine's *Step by Wicked Step* (Little, Brown, 1996):

> *It's a dark and stormy night, and five children on a school trip wind up in an old house, where they find a Victorian boy's diary.*

Cooper's choice of words ("dark and stormy night") suggests that the book has the sort of formulaic elements of spookiness that many children crave, and that the story itself is gripping from page one.

Another technique for an opening is to launch right into a critical analysis and then go on to use descriptive statements as examples. This is how Betsy Hearne approaches Julius Lester and Jerry Pinkney's new version of "Little Black Sambo," entitled *Sam and the Tigers* (Dial, 1996).

> *For living such a long and argufied life, Little Black Sambo sure looks fresh here—new words coming out of his mouth, new mouth entirely, for that matter. Sam, son of Sam and Sam, all residents of Sam-sam-sa-mara, picks out his own clothes at the bazaar, thank you. "Uh uh. That ain't me," he tells his mother,*

who's holding up a conservative
brown jacket and white shirt.

Note that Hearne's words do double duty, providing description and analysis simultaneously. For example, her observation that Sam has a "new mouth entirely" draws a subtle comparison to the offensive stereotypical depiction of Little Black Sambo's large, ruby-red lips in the original Bannerman edition. Her prose style also echoes the playful nature of Julius Lester's retelling to give readers a clear sense of the book's essence.

No matter what sort of opening you use, your review should include a mix of descriptive and analytical statements, so that readers will know what the book is about and what you thought of it. It should be clear to them whether you recommend the book or not. Do not be afraid to express your opinion, as long as you can back it up with evidence from the book.

Many readers, particularly librarians and teachers, appreciate comments about a book's popular appeal or suggestions of how it might be shared with children. They like to know if a novel would make a good classroom read-aloud for fourth graders or whether a picture book would work well in a toddler story hour. Be as specific as possible. Comments such as "Will appeal to everyone" are meaningless, while "Will appeal to Matt Christopher fans" tells readers something definite about the subject, scope, and reading level. Of course, you don't have to make predictions about a book's appeal, and it would be better to say nothing at all than to make vague or inaccurate guesses.

REVISING AND REFINING

Once you have the first rough draft down on paper, read it over critically. Is there too much description? Not enough? Did you forget to mention something important? Do you notice anything in it that is clever for its own sake? Or is the review simply too long?

Take a look at how your sentences are structured. Can any of them be condensed and combined? Look for any forms of the verb "to be"—a weak verb (unless you're Shakespeare). If you can replace it with a strong one, you will improve your review by saying the same thing in fewer words. For example:

> *Amelia is an independent girl who wants to be a airline pilot when she grows up.*

can be changed to:

> *Independent Amelia plans to fly planes one day.*

Look for redundancies. Have you said the same thing in two different ways? In the above example, I was able to delete the word "girl" because the character's personal name makes her gender clear. When you are reviewing a nonfiction book, its title often specifies content that you do not need to repeat. David Macaulay's *The Way Things Work: From Levers to Lasers, Cars to Computers—A Visual Guide to the World of Machines* provides a good example.

If you feel that your writing is perfect and the review is still too long, you are simply going to have to cut out a sentence or two. Read the review over one more time to find the lines that can be deleted without losing an important point or aspect.

The skill with which Roger Sutton, Ilene Cooper, and Betsy Hearne write reviews comes from their years of experience as professional reviewers and writers. Each one writes with a distinctive style that owes its liveliness to the use of clear, simple English. As a novice reviewer you may find it helpful to read and analyze their reviews (and those of other professional reviewers), thinking critically about how they structure them and noting the verbs and adjectives they use. With practice, experience, and perseverance, you will sharpen your own skills.

The critic John Rowe Townsend says, "Good reviewers of children's books are probably scarcer than good writers of them. And it is almost as necessary that there should be good and effective writing about children's books as that there should be good children's books. Conceivably, indeed, it is necessary in order that there should continue to *be* good children's books."

Welcome.

Source Notes and Bibliography

CHAPTER 1:
A CRITICAL APPROACH TO CHILDREN'S BOOKS

CITATIONS

Helen Roney Sattler quote p. 15 from *Hominids: A Look Back at Our Ancestors*, p. vi.

SOURCES

Briley, Dorothy. "The Impact of Reviewing on Children's Book Publishing," in *Evaluating Children's Books: A Critical Look*, edited by Betsy Hearne and Roger Sutton. Papers presented at the Allerton Park Institute, No. 34. Urbana–Champaign, IL: University of Illinois, 1993, pp. 105–17.

Dessauer, John P. *Book Publishing: A Basic Introduction*. New expanded edition. New York: Continuum, 1989.

Giblin, James Cross. *Writing Books for Young People*. Boston: The Writer, 1990.

Karl, Jean E. *How to Write and Sell Children's Picture Books.* Cincinnati, OH: Writer's Digest, 1994.

Litowinsky, Olga. *Writing and Publishing Books for Children in the 1990s: The Inside Story from the Editor's Desk.* New York: Walker, 1992.

McElderry, Margaret K. "Remarkable Women: Anne Carroll Moore & Company," *School Library Journal* 38:3 (March 1992), pp. 156–62.

McNamara, Shelley G. "Early Public Library Work with Children," *Top of the News* 43:1 (Fall 1986), pp. 59–72.

CHILDREN'S BOOKS CITED

Cole, Joanna. *How You Were Born.* New York: Morrow, 1993.

Sattler, Helen Roney. *Hominids: A Look Back at Our Ancestors.* Illustrated by Christopher Santoro. New York: Lothrop, 1988.

St. George, Judith. *Crazy Horse.* New York: Putnam, 1994.

CHAPTER 2:
BOOKS OF INFORMATION

CITATIONS

Laurence Pringle quote p. 37 from *Being a Plant,* p. 54.

David Macaulay quote p. 38 from *The Way Things Work,* p. 31.

Helen Roney Sattler quote p. 39 from *Hominids: A Look Back at Our Ancestors,* p. 46.

Milton Meltzer quote p. 40 from "Beyond Fact," in *Beyond Fact:*

Nonfiction for Children and Young People, edited by Jo Carr, p. 30.

Walter Dean Myers quote p. 40 from *Now Is Your Time: The African-American Struggle for Freedom*, p. 71.

SOURCES

Broadway, Marsha D., and Malia Howland. "Science Books for Young People: Who Writes Them?" *School Library Journal* 37:5 (May 1991), pp. 35–38.

Carr, Jo. *Beyond Fact: Nonfiction for Children and Young People*. Chicago, IL: American Library Association, 1982.

Carter, Betty. "Reviewing Nonfiction for Children: Stance, Scholarship and Structure," in *Evaluating Children's Books: A Critical Look*, edited by Betsy Hearne and Roger Sutton. Papers presented at the Allerton Park Institute, No. 34. Urbana–Champaign, IL: University of Illinois, 1993, pp. 59–71.

Carter, Betty, and Richard F. Abrahamson. *Nonfiction for Young Adults: From Delight to Wisdom*. Phoenix, AZ: Oryx Press, 1990.

Epstein, Connie C. "Accuracy in Nonfiction," *School Library Journal* 33:7 (March 1987), pp. 113–15.

Giblin, James Cross. "The Rise & Fall & Rise of Juvenile Nonfiction, 1961–1988," *School Library Journal* 35:2 (October 1988), pp. 27–31.

Meltzer, Milton. "Where Do All the Prizes Go?: The Case for Nonfiction," *The Horn Book* 52:1 (February 1976), pp. 17–23.

Millhouser, Frances. "Beautiful Science: Books That Cash In on

Children's Curiosity," *School Library Journal* 37:5 (May 1991), pp. 47–48.

CHILDREN'S BOOKS CITED

Arnosky, Jim. *Drawing Life in Motion*. New York: Lothrop, 1984.

Bierhorst, John. *The Hungry Woman: Myths and Legends of the Aztecs*. With illustrations by Aztec artists of the sixteenth century. New York: Morrow, 1984.

Blumberg, Rhoda. *Commodore Perry in the Land of the Shogun*. New York: Lothrop, 1985.

Cole, Joanna. *The Magic School Bus Lost in the Solar System*. Illustrated by Bruce Degen. New York: Scholastic, 1990.

Freedman, Russell. *Lincoln: A Photobiography*. Illustrated with photographs and prints. New York: Clarion, 1987.

Fritz, Jean. *You Want Women to Vote, Lizzie Stanton?* Illustrated by DyAnne Di Salvo-Ryan. New York: Putnam, 1995.

Giblin, James Cross. *From Hand to Mouth: Or, How We Invented Knives, Forks, Spoons, and Chopsticks & the Table Manners To Go With Them*. Illustrated with photographs, prints, and drawings. New York: Crowell, 1987.

Komori, Atsushi. *Animal Mothers*. Illustrated by Masayuki Yabuuchi. New York: Philomel, 1979.

Kuklin, Susan. *Kodomo: Children of Japan*. New York: Putnam, 1995.

Lasky, Kathryn. *Sugaring Time*. Photographs by Christopher Knight. New York: Macmillan, 1983.

Lauber, Patricia. *The News About Dinosaurs*. Illustrated by

Gregory S. Paul, Douglas Henderson, Mark Hallett, John Gurche, Robert T. Bakker, *et al.* New York: Bradbury, 1989.

———. *Volcano: The Eruption and Healing of Mount St. Helens.* New York: Bradbury, 1986.

Lavies, Bianca. *Compost Critters.* New York: Dutton, 1993.

Macaulay, David. *The Way Things Work: From Levers to Lasers, Cars to Computers—A Visual Guide to the World of Machines.* Boston: Houghton Mifflin, 1988.

Macy, Sue. *A Whole New Ball Game: The Story of the All-American Girls Professional Baseball League.* New York: Henry Holt, 1993.

Meltzer, Milton. *Never to Forget: The Jews of the Holocaust.* New York: Harper, 1976.

———. *Poverty in America.* New York: Morrow, 1986.

Myers, Walter Dean. *Now Is Your Time: The African-American Struggle for Freedom.* New York: Harper, 1991.

Pringle, Laurence. *Being a Plant.* Illustrations by Robin Brickman. New York: Crowell, 1983.

Rogers, Fred. *Going to Day Care.* Photographs by Jim Judkis. New York: Putnam, 1985.

———. *Going to the Doctor.* Photographs by Jim Judkis. New York: Putnam, 1986.

———. *Making Friends.* Photographs by Jim Judkis. New York: Putnam, 1987.

Sattler, Helen Roney. *Hominids: A Look Back at Our Ancestors.* Illustrated by Christopher Santoro. New York: Lothrop, 1988.

Simon, Seymour. *Our Solar System.* New York: Morrow, 1992.

Turner, Glennette Tilley. *Lewis Howard Latimer*. Englewood Cliffs, NJ: Silver Burdett, 1991.

CHAPTER 3: TRADITIONAL LITERATURE

CITATIONS

Betsy Hearne quote p. 53 from "Cite the Source: Reducing Cultural Chaos in Picture Books, Part One," p. 27.

Kevin Crossley-Holland quotes pp. 54–55 from *British Folk Tales: New Versions*, p. 374.

James Marshall quote p. 56 from *Goldilocks and the Three Bears*, p. [14].

Julius Lester quote p. 57 from *John Henry*, p. [10].

Paul Goble quote p. 58 from *Iktomi and the Boulder*, p. 5.

John Bierhorst quote p. 59 from *The White Deer, and Other Stories Told by the Lenape*, p. 21.

Joseph Bruchac quote p. 59 from *The Girl Who Married the Moon: Tales from Native North America*, p. 29.

Jane Kurtz quote p. 65 from "Multicultural Children's Books: The Subtle Tug-of-War," p. 41.

SOURCES

Andrews, Loretta Kreider. Review of *Pulling the Lion's Tale* by Jane Kurtz, *School Library Journal* 41:12 (December 1995), pp. 83–84.

Hearne, Betsy. "Cite the Source: Reducing Cultural Chaos in Picture Books, Part One," *School Library Journal* 39:7 (July 1993), pp. 22–27.

―――. "Respect the Source: Reducing Cultural Chaos in Picture Books, Part Two," *School Library Journal* 39:8 (August 1993), pp. 33–37.

Kurtz, Jane. Letter to the Editor, *School Library Journal* 42:1 (January 1996), p. 74.

―――. "Multicultural Children's Books: The Subtle Tug-of-War," *School Library Journal* 42:2 (February 1995), pp. 40–41.

Miller-Lachmann, Lyn. "Multicultural Publishing: The Folktale Flood," *School Library Journal* 40:2 (February 1994), pp. 35–36.

Opie, Iona and Peter. *The Classic Fairy Tales.* London: Oxford University Press, 1974.

Scheps, Susan. Review of *The Lion's Whiskers* by Nancy Raines Day, *School Library Journal* 41:4 (April 1995), pp. 140–41.

Yeh, Phoebe. "Multicultural Publishing: The Best and the Worst of Times," *Journal of Youth Services in Libraries* 6:2 (Winter 1993), pp. 157–60.

Yohannes, Gebregeorgis. Letter to the Editor, *School Library Journal* 42:4 (April 1996), p. 98.

CHILDREN'S BOOKS CITED

Barton, Byron. *The Three Bears.* New York: Harper, 1991.

Bierhorst, John. *The White Deer, and Other Stories Told by the Lenape.* New York: Morrow, 1995.

Bruchac, Joseph, and Gayle Ross. *The Girl Who Married the Moon: Tales from Native North America.* Mahwah, NJ: Bridgewater, 1994.

Crossley-Holland, Kevin. *British Folk Tales: New Versions.* New York: Orchard, 1987.

Day, Nancy Raines. *The Lion's Whiskers: An Ethiopian Folktale.* Illustrated by Ann Grifalconi. New York: Scholastic, 1995.

Goble, Paul. *Iktomi and the Boulder.* New York: Orchard, 1988.

Grimm, Jakob and Wilhelm. *Hansel and Gretel.* Translated from the German by Elizabeth D. Crawford. Illustrated by Lisbeth Zwerger. New York: Morrow, 1979.

———. *Hansel and Gretel.* Translated by Mrs. Edgar Lucas. Illustrated by Susan Jeffers. New York: Dial, 1980.

———. *Hansel and Gretel.* Adapted from the translation by Eleanor Quarrie. Illustrated by Anthony Browne. New York: Franklin Watts, 1981.

———. *Hansel and Gretel.* Translated and retold by Rika Lesser. Illustrated by Paul O. Zelinsky. New York: Dodd, Mead, 1984.

Hamilton, Virginia. *In the Beginning: Creation Stories from Around the World.* Illustrated by Barry Moser. New York: Harcourt, 1988.

Kurtz, Jane. *Pulling the Lion's Tale.* Illustrated by Floyd Cooper. New York: Simon & Schuster, 1995.

Lester, Julius. *John Henry.* Illustrated by Jerry Pinkney. New York: Dial, 1994.

Marshall, James. *Goldilocks and the Three Bears.* New York: Dial, 1988.

Schwartz, Alvin. *In a Dark, Dark Room and Other Scary Stories*. Illustrated by Dirk Zimmer. (An I Can Read Book) New York: Harper, 1984.

———. *Scary Stories to Tell in the Dark: Collected from American Folklore*. Illustrated by Stephen Gammell. New York: Harper, 1981.

Vuong, Lynette Dyer, and Manabu Saito. *The Golden Carp, and Other Tales from Vietnam*. New York: Lothrop, 1993.

CHAPTER 4: POETRY, VERSE, RHYMES, AND SONGS

CITATIONS

Karla Kuskin poem "Thistles" p. 71 from *Dogs & Dragons, Trees & Dreams*, p. 4.

Eloise Greenfield poem "Lessie" p. 72 from *Honey, I Love and Other Love Poems*, p. [34].

Arnold Adoff poem p. 73 from *i am the running girl*, p. [33].

Gwendolyn Brooks poem "Cynthia in the Snow" p. 74 from *Bronzeville Boys and Girls*, p. 8.

Iona and Peter Opie quote p. 76 from *The Oxford Dictionary of Nursery Rhymes*, p. 1.

X. J. Kennedy poem "Lighting a Fire" p. 80 from *The Forgetful Wishing Well*, p. 52.

SOURCES

Copeland, Jeffrey S. *Speaking of Poets: Interviews with Poets Who Write for Children and Young Adults.* Urbana, IL: National Council of Teachers of English, 1993.

Deutsch, Babette. *Poetry Handbook: A Dictionary of Terms.* Fourth Edition. New York: Harper, 1974.

England, Claire, and Adele Fasick. *Childview: Evaluating and Reviewing Materials for Children.* Littleton, CO: Libraries Unlimited, 1987.

Korbeck, Sharon. "Children's Poetry: Journeying Beyond the Road Less Traveled," *School Library Journal* 41:4 (April 1995), pp. 43–44.

Lukens, Rebecca J. *A Critical Handbook of Children's Literature.* Second edition. Oxford, OH: Scott, Foresman, 1982.

Opie, Iona and Peter. *The Oxford Dictionary of Nursery Rhymes.* Oxford: Oxford University Press, 1952.

Schliesman, Megan. "Poetry for All Seasons and Many Reasons: Selected from *CCBC Choices* 1990–1995." Selected bibliography compiled, printed, and distributed by the Cooperative Children's Book Center, Madison, Wisconsin. April 1996.

Whalin, Kathleen. "Becoming Versed in Poetry," *School Library Journal* 42:4 (April 1996), pp. 38–39.

CHILDREN'S BOOKS CITED

Adoff, Arnold. *i am the running girl.* Illustrated by Ronald Himler. New York: Harper, 1979.

Brooks, Gwendolyn. *Bronzeville Boys and Girls.* Illustrated by Ronni Solbert. New York: Harper, 1956.

Bryan, Ashley. *All Night, All Day: A Child's First Book of African-American Spirituals.* New York: Atheneum, 1991.

Cole, William. *A Book of Nature Poems.* New York: Viking, 1969.

Cousins, Lucy. *The Little Dog Laughed, and Other Nursery Rhymes.* New York: Dutton, 1990.

Fleischman, Paul. *Joyful Noise: Poems for Two Voices.* Illustrated by Eric Beddows. New York: Charlotte Zolotow/Harper, 1988.

Greenfield, Eloise. *Honey I Love and Other Love Poems.* New York: Crowell, 1978.

Hale, Sarah Josepha. *Mary Had a Little Lamb.* Photographs by Bruce MacMillan. New York: Scholastic, 1990.

Hopkins, Lee Bennett. *Surprises.* Illustrated by Megan Lloyd. (An I Can Read Book) New York: Charlotte Zolotow/Harper, 1984.

Kennedy, X. J. *The Forgetful Wishing Well.* Illustrated by Monica Incisa. New York: Margaret K. McElderry/ Atheneum, 1985.

Kuskin, Karla. *Dogs & Dragons, Trees & Dreams.* New York: Harper 1980. Poem originally published in *The Rose on My Cake* (Harper, 1964).

Langstaff, John. *Frog Went A-Courtin'.* Illustrated by Feodor Rojankovsky. New York: Harcourt, 1955.

———. *Hi! Ho! The Rattling Bog, and Other Folk Songs for Group Singing.* New York: Harcourt, 1969.

Lobel, Arnold. *The Random House Book of Mother Goose: A Treasury of 306 Timeless Nursery Rhymes.* New York: Random House, 1986.

Marshall, James. *Old Mother Hubbard and Her Wonderful Dog*. New York: Farrar, Straus, 1991.

Mattox, Cheryl Warren. *Shake It to the One That You Love the Best: Play Songs and Lullabies from Black Musical Traditions*. Illustrated by Varnette P. Honeywood and Brenda Joysmith. San Mateo, CA: Warren-Mattox, 1990.

Moore, Lilian. *Sunflakes: Poems for Children*. Illustrated by Jan Ormerod. New York: Clarion, 1992.

Opie, Iona and Peter. *Tail Feathers from Mother Goose: The Opie Rhyme Book*. Boston: Little, Brown, 1988.

Silverstein, Shel. *Falling Up*. New York: Harper, 1996.

———. *A Light in the Attic*. New York: Harper, 1981.

———. *Where the Sidewalk Ends*. New York: Harper, 1974.

Soto, Gary. *Neighborhood Odes*. Illustrated by David Diaz. San Diego: Harcourt, 1992.

Sutherland, Zena. *The Orchard Book of Nursery Rhymes*. Illustrated by Faith Jaques. New York: Orchard, 1990.

Worth, Valerie. *Small Poems*. Illustrated by Natalie Babbit. New York: Farrar, Straus, 1972.

CHAPTER 5: PICTURE BOOKS

CITATIONS

Dilys Evans quote p. 89 from "An Extraordinary Vision: Picture Books of the Nineties," p. 759.

Margaret Wise Brown quote p. 92 from *The Indoor Noisy Book*, p. [14].

Margaret Wise Brown quote p. 96 from *The Runaway Bunny*, pp. [8–13].

Margaret Wise Brown quote p. 98 from *The Little Island*, pp. [9–17].

Timothy M. Rivinus and Lisa Audet quote p. 108 from "The Psychological Genius of Margaret Wise Brown," p. 10.

SOURCES

Bader, Barbara. *American Picture Books from Noah's Ark to the Beast Within.* New York: Macmillan, 1976.

Bechtel, Louise Seaman. "Margaret Wise Brown: Laureate of the Nursery," *Horn Book* 34:3 (June 1958), pp. 173–86.

Behrmann, Christine. "The Media Used in Caldecott Medal Picture Books: Notes Toward a Definitive List," *Journal of Youth Services in Libraries* 1:2 (Winter 1988), pp. 198–212.

Cianciolo, Patricia J. *Picture Books for Children.* Third edition. Chicago: American Library Association, 1990.

Couch, Tony. *Tony Couch's Keys to Successful Painting.* Cincinnati, OH: North Light, 1992.

Evans, Dilys. "An Extraordinary Vision," *Horn Book* 67:6 (November/December 1991), pp. 712–15.

———. "An Extraordinary Vision: Picture Books of the Nineties," *Horn Book* 68:6 (November/December 1992), pp. 759–63.

Griffith, Thomas. *A Practical Guide for Beginning Painters.* Englewood Cliffs, NJ: Prentice Hall, 1981.

Hands, Nancy. *Illustrating Children's Books: A Guide to*

Drawing, Printing, and Publishing. New York: Prentice Hall, 1986.

Henkes, Kevin. "Illustration in Children's Books: Printmaking Techniques." Selected bibliography compiled, printed, and distributed by the Cooperative Children's Book Center, Madison, Wisconsin. May 1982.

Karl, Jean E. *How to Write and Sell Children's Picture Books.* Cincinnati, OH: Writer's Digest, 1994.

Kiefer, Barbara. "Visual Criticism and Children's Literature," in *Evaluating Children's Books: A Critical Look*, edited by Betsy Hearne and Roger Sutton. Papers presented at the Allerton Park Institute, No. 34. Urbana–Champaign, IL: University of Illinois, 1993, pp. 73–91.

Lacy, Lyn Ellen. *Art and Design in Children's Picture Books: An Analysis of Caldecott Award–Winning Illustrations.* Chicago: American Library Association, 1986.

Lurie, Stephanie. "First the Word: An Editor's View of Picture Book Texts," *School Library Journal* 37:10 (October 1991), pp. 50–51.

McCann, Donnarae, and Olga Richard. *The Child's First Books: A Critical Study of Pictures and Texts.* New York: Wilson, 1973.

Marantz, Sylvia and Kenneth. "Interview with Paul O. Zelinsky," *Horn Book* 62:3 (May/June 1986), pp. 295–304.

Marcus, Leonard S. *Margaret Wise Brown: Awakened by the Moon.* Boston: Beacon Press, 1992.

Mitchell, Lucy Sprague. *Two Lives: The Story of Wesley Clair Mitchell and Myself.* New York: Simon & Schuster, 1953.

Osterweil, Wendy. "Drawing in Children's Book Illustration." Selected bibliography compiled, printed, and distributed by the Cooperative Children's Book Center, Madison, Wisconsin. May 1985.

———. "Painting Media in Children's Book Illustration." Selected bibliography compiled, printed, and distributed by the Cooperative Children's Book Center, Madison, Wisconsin. June 1984.

Rivinus, Timothy M., and Lisa Audet. "The Psychological Genius of Margaret Wise Brown," *Children's Literature in Education* 23:1 (March 1992), pp. 1–14.

Shulevitz, Uri. *Writing with Pictures: How to Write and Illustrate Children's Books.* New York: Watson-Guptill, 1985.

Stewig, John Warren. *Looking at Picture Books.* Fort Atkinson, WI: Highsmith Press, 1995.

CHILDREN'S BOOKS CITED

Baker, Olaf. *Where the Buffaloes Begin.* Illustrated by Stephen Gammell. New York: Frederick Warne, 1981.

Bang, Molly. *Ten Nine Eight.* New York: Greenwillow, 1983.

Brown, Margaret Wise. *Goodnight Moon.* Illustrated by Clement Hurd. New York: Harper, 1947.

———. *The Indoor Noisy Book.* Illustrated by Leonard Weisgard. New York: Harper, 1942.

———. *The Runaway Bunny.* Illustrated by Clement Hurd. New York: Harper, 1942.

——— (writing under the pseudonym Golden MacDonald). *The Little Island.* Illustrated by Leonard Weisgard. New York: Doubleday, 1946.

Browne, Anthony. *Changes.* New York: Knopf, 1990.

Bryan, Ashley. *All Night, All Day: A Child's First Book of African-American Spirituals.* New York: Atheneum, 1991.

Burton, Virginia Lee. *The Little House.* Boston: Houghton, Mifflin, 1943.

Crews, Nina. *One Hot Summer Day.* New York: Greenwillow, 1995.

Dorros, Arthur. *Tonight Is Carnaval.* Illustrated with *arpilleras* sewn by the Club de Madres Virgen del Carmen of Lima, Peru. New York: Dutton, 1991.

Gág, Wanda. *Millions of Cats.* New York: Coward-McCann, 1928.

Geisert, Arthur. *After the Flood.* Boston: Houghton Mifflin, 1994.

———. *The Ark.* Boston: Houghton, Mifflin, 1988.

Griffith, Helen V. *Grandaddy's Place.* Illustrated by James Stevenson. New York: Greenwillow, 1987.

Grimm, Jakob and Wilhelm. *Hansel and Gretel.* Translated and retold by Rika Lesser. Illustrated by Paul O. Zelinsky. New York: Dodd, Mead, 1984.

Hall, Donald. *Ox-Cart Man.* Illustrated by Barbara Cooney. New York: Viking, 1979.

Lester, Julius. *John Henry.* Illustrated by Jerry Pinkney. New York: Dial, 1994.

Levine, Ellen. *I Hate English!* Illustrated by Steve Björkman. New York: Scholastic, 1989.

Lionni, Leo. *Tico and the Golden Wings.* New York: Pantheon, 1964.

Noble, Trinka Hakes. *The Day Jimmy's Boa Ate the Wash.* Illustrated by Steven Kellogg. New York: Dial, 1980.

O'Kelley, Mattie Lou. *From the Hills of Georgia: An Autobiography in Paintings.* Boston: Little, Brown, 1983.

Raschka, Chris. *Yo! Yes?* New York: Orchard, 1993.

Rathmann, Peggy. *Officer Buckle and Gloria.* New York: Putnam, 1995.

Rylant, Cynthia. *The Relatives Came.* Illustrated by Stephen Gammell. Scarsdale, NY: Bradbury, 1985.

San Souci, Robert D. *The Faithful Friend.* Illustrated by Brian Pinkney. New York: Simon & Schuster, 1995.

Steig, William. *Doctor De Soto.* New York: Farrar, Straus, 1982.

Steptoe, John. *Mufaro's Beautiful Daughters.* New York: Lothrop, 1987.

Stevenson, James. *There's Nothing to Do.* New York: Greenwillow, 1986.

Trezise, Percy, and Dick Roughsey. *Gidja the Moon.* Milwaukee, WI: Gareth Stevens, 1988.

Van Allsburg, Chris. *The Wreck of the Zephyr.* Boston: Houghton Mifflin, 1983.

Williams, Vera B. *A Chair for My Mother.* New York: Greenwillow, 1982.

———. *More More More, Said the Baby: 3 Love Stories.* New York: Greenwillow, 1990.

Xiong, Blia. *Nine-in-One Grr! Grr!: A Folktale from the Hmong People of Laos.* Adapted by Cathy Spagnoli. Illustrated by Nancy Hom. San Francisco: Children's Book Press, 1989.

Young, Ed. *Seven Blind Mice.* New York: Philomel, 1992.

Zolotow, Charlotte. *Mr. Rabbit and the Lovely Present.* Illustrated by Maurice Sendak. New York: Harper, 1962.

CHAPTER 6:
EASY READERS AND
TRANSITIONAL BOOKS

CITATIONS

John Hersey quote p. 122 from: "Why Do Students Bog Down with the First R?: A Local Community Sheds Light on a National Problem: Reading," p. 148.

Arnold Lobel quote p. 123 from *Frog and Toad Are Friends*, pp. 20–24.

Dr. Seuss quote p. 133 from *The Cat in the Hat*, p. 25.

Edward Marshall quote p. 131 from *Three by the Sea*, pp. 38–39.

Else Holmelund Minarik quote p. 131 from *Little Bear*, p. 24.

Peggy Parish quote p. 132 from *Dinosaur Time*, p. 5.

P. D. Eastman quote p. 139 from *Are You My Mother?*, p. 62.

Molly Garrett Bang quote p. 140 from *Wiley and the Hairy Man*, pp. 12–13.

Sue Alexander quote p. 141 from *Witch, Goblin and Ghost Are Back*, pp. 58–59.

Ann Cameron quote p. 144 from *The Stories Julian Tells*, p. 37.

Ellen Conford quote p. 144 from *A Job for Jenny Archer*, p. 6.

S. E. Hinton quote p. 145 from *The Puppy Sister*, p. 2.

Clyde Robert Bulla quotes p. 147 from *The Chalk Box Kid*, pp. 5, 29, 51.

SOURCES

Adams, Marilyn Jager. *Beginning to Read: Thinking and*

Learning About Print. Cambridge, MA: MIT Press, 1990.

Barstow, Barbara, and Judith Riggle. *Beyond Picture Books: A Guide to First Readers.* Second edition. New Providence, NJ: Bowker, 1995.

Hersey, John. "Why Do Students Bog Down with the First R?: A Local Community Sheds Light on a National Problem: Reading," *Life* 36:21 (May 24, 1954), pp. 136–50.

Jensen, Margaret. "Books for Beginning Readers: A Bibliography of Trade Books for Young Children." Selected bibliography compiled, printed, and distributed by the Cooperative Children's Book Center, Madison, Wisconsin. April 1984.

———. "Characteristics of Trade Books." Books for Beginning Readers Workshop, May 3, 1984 (audiotape). Cooperative Children's Book Center, University of Wisconsin—Madison.

———, Kathleen T. Horning, Ginny Moore Kruse, and Deana Grobe. "Young Fiction: Books for Transitional Readers." Selected bibliography compiled, printed, and distributed by the Cooperative Children's Book Center, Madison, Wisconsin. April 1989.

McDonald, Ruth. *Dr. Seuss.* Boston: Twayne, 1988.

Mogilner, Alijandra. *Children's Writer's Word Book.* Cincinnati, OH: Writer's Digest, 1992.

CHILDREN'S BOOKS CITED

Alexander, Sue. *Witch, Goblin and Ghost Are Back.* Illustrated by Jeanette Winter. (I Am Reading Stories) New York: Pantheon, 1985.

Bang, Molly Garrett. *Wiley and the Hairy Man: Adapted from an American Folk Tale.* (Ready-to-Read) New York: Macmillan, 1976.

Bulla, Clyde Robert. *The Chalk Box Kid.* Illustrated by Thomas B. Allen. (A Stepping Stone Book) New York: Random House, 1987.

Byars, Betsy. *Beans on the Roof.* Illustrated by Melodye Rosales. New York: Delacorte, 1988.

Cameron, Ann. *Julian's Glorious Summer.* Illustrated by Dora Leder. (A Stepping Stone Book) New York: Random House, 1987.

———. *More Stories Julian Tells.* Illustrated by Ann Strugnell. New York: Knopf, 1986.

———. *The Stories Julian Tells.* Illustrated by Ann Strugnell. New York: Pantheon, 1981.

Conford, Ellen. *A Job for Jenny Archer.* Illustrated by Diane Palmisciano. (A Springboard Book) Boston: Little, Brown, 1989.

Eastman, P. D. *Are You My Mother?* (Beginner Books) New York: Random House, 1960.

Hinton, S. E. *The Puppy Sister.* Illustrated by Jacqueline Rogers. New York: Delacorte, 1995.

Howe, James. *Pinky and Rex and the Bully.* Illustrated by Melissa Sweet. (Ready-to-Read: Level 3) New York: Atheneum, 1996.

Korschunow, Irina. *Adam Draws Himself a Dragon.* Translated from the German by James Skofield. Illustrated by Mary Rahn. New York: Harper, 1986.

Lobel, Arnold. *Frog and Toad Are Friends.* (An I Can Read Book) New York: Harper, 1970.

Marshall, Edward. *Three by the Sea*. Illustrated by James
      Marshall. (Dial Easy-to-Read) New York: Dial, 1981.
Minarik, Else Holmelund. *Little Bear*. Illustrated by Maurice
      Sendak. (An I Can Read Book) New York: Harper, 1957.
Parish, Peggy. *Dinosaur Time*. Illustrated by Arnold Lobel. (An
      I Can Read Book) New York: Harper, 1974.
Rylant, Cynthia. *Henry and Mudge: The First Book*. Illustrated
      by Suçie Stevenson. New York: Bradbury, 1987.
Seuss, Dr. *The Cat in the Hat*. (Beginner Books) New York:
      Random House, 1957.

CHAPTER 7: FICTION

CITATIONS

Anne Carroll Moore quote p. 150 from *My Roads to Childhood:
      Views and Reviews of Children's Books*, p. 23.
Louise P. Latimer quote p. 151 from "They Who Get Slapped," p.
      626.
Karen Cushman quotes pp. 162, 163, 164 from *The Midwife's
      Apprentice*, pp. 1–2, 7, 31, 32, 36.
Kevin Henkes quotes pp. 169, 170, 171 from *Words of Stone*, pp.
      17, 77, 52, 7, 1, 113, 151, 85, 84, 40, 116, 23, 41, 40.
Virginia Hamilton quote p. 172 from *Sweet Whispers, Brother
      Rush*, p. 9.
Virginia Hamilton quote p. 173 from *The Magical Adventures of
      Pretty Pearl*, p. 71.

SOURCES

England, Claire, and Adele Fasick. *Childview: Evaluating and Reviewing Materials for Children.* Littleton, CO: Libraries Unlimited, 1987.

Latimer, Louise P. "They Who Get Slapped," *Library Journal* 49:13 (July 1924) pp. 623–26.

Lukens, Rebecca J. *A Critical Handbook of Children's Literature.* Second edition. Oxford, OH: Scott, Foresman, 1982.

Moore, Anne Carroll. *My Roads to Childhood: Views and Reviews of Children's Books.* New York: Doubleday, 1939.

Vandegrift, Kay E. *Child and Story: The Literary Connection.* New York: Neal-Schuman, 1980.

CHILDREN'S BOOKS CITED

Avi. *Nothing but the Truth: A Documentary Novel.* New York: Orchard, 1991.

Creech, Sharon. *Walk Two Moons.* New York: Harper, 1994.

Cushman, Karen. *The Midwife's Apprentice.* New York: Clarion, 1995.

Farmer, Nancy. *The Ear, the Eye and the Arm.* New York: Orchard, 1994.

Fleischman, Paul. *Bull Run.* New York: Laura Geringer/Harper, 1993.

Hamilton, Virginia. *The Magical Adventures of Pretty Pearl.* New York: Charlotte Zolotow/Harper, 1983.

———. *Sweet Whispers, Brother Rush.* New York: Philomel, 1982.

Henkes, Kevin. *Words of Stone.* New York: Greenwillow, 1992.

Lowry, Lois. *Anastasia Krupnik.* Boston: Houghton Mifflin, 1979.

———. *Number the Stars.* Boston: Houghton Mifflin, 1989.

Myers, Walter Dean. *Scorpions.* New York: Harper, 1988.

Paterson, Katherine. *Jacob Have I Loved.* New York: Crowell, 1980.

Paulsen, Gary. *Hatchet.* Scarsdale, NY: Bradbury, 1987.

Taylor, Mildred D. *Roll of Thunder, Hear My Cry.* New York: Dial, 1976.

Vail, Rachel. *Daring to Be Abigail.* New York: Orchard, 1996.

CHAPTER 8:
WRITING A REVIEW

CITATIONS

Virginia Woolf quote p. 176 from "Reviewing," in *The Captain's Death Bed, and Other Essays,* p. 130.

Paul Heins quotes p. 179 from "Out on a Limb with the Critics: Some Random Thoughts on the Present State of the Criticism of Children's Literature," pp. 269, 268.

Phyllis K. Kennemer quote p. 186 from "Reviews of Fiction Books: How They Differ," p. 419.

Betsy Hearne quote p. 188 from "A Reviewer's Story," p. 82.

Zena Sutherland quote p. 188 from "A Life in Review," p. 360.

Kathleen T. Horning quote p. 189 from review of *Shortcut* by David Macaulay, Milwaukee *Journal Sentinel,* November 14, 1995.

Roger Sutton quote p. 190 from review of *Granny the Pag* by Nina Bawden.

Ilene Cooper quote p. 191 from review of *Step by Wicked Step* by Anne Fine.

Betsy Hearne quote p. 191 from review of *Sam and the Tigers: A New Telling of Little Black Sambo* by Julius Lester.

John Rowe Townsend quote p. 194 from "The Reviewing of Children's Books," in *Celebrating Children's Books: Essays on Children's Literature in Honor of Zena Sutherland,* p. 187.

SOURCES

Cooper, Ilene. Review of *Step By Wicked Step* by Anne Fine. *Booklist* 92:16 (May 15, 1996), p. 1588.

Craver, Kathleen W. "Book Reviewers: An Empirical Portrait," *School Library Media Quarterly* 12:5 (Fall 1984), pp. 383–409.

Darling, Richard L. *The Rise of Children's Book Reviewing in America, 1865–1881.* New York: Bowker, 1968.

Drewry, John E. *Writing Book Reviews.* Boston: The Writer, 1966.

Elleman, Barbara. "A Sentimental Journey," *Booklist* 81:21 (July 1985), p. 1551.

Hearne, Betsy. Review of *Sam and the Tigers: A New Telling of Little Black Sambo* by Julius Lester. *Bulletin of the Center for Children's Books* 49:11 (July/August 1996), p. 378.

———. "A Reviewer's Story," *Library Quarterly* 51:1 (January 1981), pp. 80–87.

Heins, Paul. "Out on a Limb with the Critics: Some Random Thoughts on the Present State of the Criticism of Children's Literature," *Horn Book* 46:3 (June 1970), pp. 264–73.

Horning, Kathleen T. Review of *Shortcut* by David Macaulay, Milwaukee *Journal Sentinel,* November 14, 1995, p. 4E.

Kammerman, Sylvia E. *Book Reviewing.* Boston: The Writer, 1978.

Kennemer, Phyllis K. "Reviews of Fiction Books: How They Differ," *Top of the News* 40:4 (Summer 1984), pp. 419–22.

McCanse, Ralph Alan. *The Art of the Book Review: A Comprehensive Working Outline.* Madison, WI: University of Wisconsin Press, 1963.

Silver, Linda R. "Criticism, Reviewing and the Library Review Media," *Top of the News* 35:2 (Winter 1979), pp. 123–30.

Sutherland, Zena. "A Life in Review," *Journal of Youth Services in Libraries* 9:4 (Summer 1996), pp. 357–65.

Sutton, Roger. Review of *Granny the Pag* by Nina Bawden. *The Bulletin of the Center for Children's Books* 49:7 (March 1996), p. 219.

Thomson, Ashley. "How to Review a Book," *Canadian Library Journal* 48:6 (December 1991), pp. 416–18.

Townsend, John Rowe. "The Reviewing of Children's Books," in *Celebrating Children's Books: Essays on Children's Literature in Honor of Zena Sutherland.* Edited by Betsy Hearne and Marilyn Kaye. New York: Lothrop, 1981, pp. 165–87.

Walford, A. J. *Reviews and Reviewing: A Guide.* Phoenix, AZ: Oryx Press, 1986.

"What Makes a Good Review? Ten Experts Speak," *Top of the News* 35:2 (Winter 1979), pp. 146–52.

Woolf, Virginia S. "Reviewing," in The *Captain's Death Bed, and Other Essays*. New York: Harcourt, 1950, pp. 127–42.

CHILDREN'S BOOKS CITED

Bannerman, Helen. *The Story of Little Black Sambo*. Philadelphia: Lippincott, 1923.

Bawden, Nina. *Granny the Pag*. New York: Clarion, 1996.

Dorris, Michael. *Sees Behind Trees*. New York: Hyperion, 1996.

Fine, Anne. *Step by Wicked Step*. Boston: Little, Brown, 1996.

Lester, Julius. *Sam and the Tigers: A New Telling of Little Black Sambo*. Illustrated by Jerry Pinkney. New York: Dial, 1996.

Macaulay, David. *Black and White*. Boston: Houghton Mifflin, 1990.

———. *Shortcut*. Boston: Houghton Mifflin, 1995.

———. *The Way Things Work: From Levers to Lasers, Cars to Computers—A Visual Guide to the World of Machines*. Boston: Houghton Mifflin, 1988.

Prelutsky, Jack. *Monday's Troll*. Illustrated by Peter Sís. New York: Greenwillow, 1996.

INDEX